"Dominator culture has tried to keep us all afraid, to make us choose safety instead of risk, sameness instead of diversity. Moving through that fear, finding out what connects us, revelling in our differences; this is the process that brings us closer, that gives us a world of shared values, of meaningful community."

~ bell hooks

Thorn & Bloom Magazine Issue 02: Breaking the Cycle
First published by redrosethorns, June 2025
This Edition published by redrosethorns, November 2025

Edited by Kirsty Anne Richards

ISBN: 979-8-9931229-1-5

Published by redrosethorns Ltd. Liability Co. (USA)
Also operating as redrosethorns Ltd. (UK)
www.redrosethorns.com

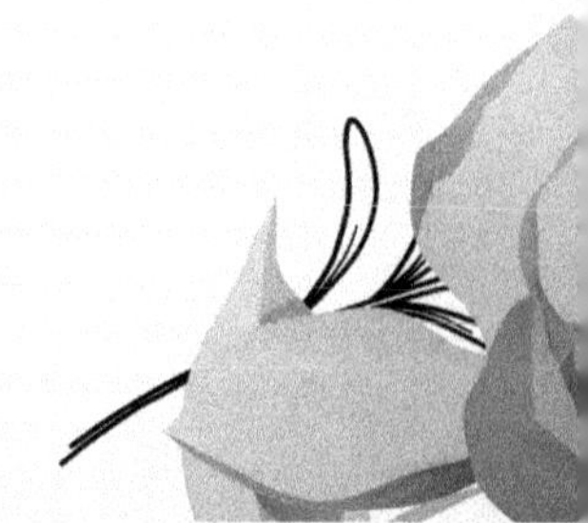

redrosethorns publishing

redrosethorns journal

Our core publication, *redrosethorns journal*, is dedicated to exploring themes of mental health, self-care, gender and sexuality, and empowerment. Through the literature we publish, we aim not only to raise awareness of these topics but also to educate, inspire, and empower our readers.

As an online journal, redrosethorns features diverse literary works across all genres and styles, released monthly. To ensure accessibility, all pieces are free to read, and our subscribers receive a featured piece each week, fostering ongoing conversations and engagement.

redrosethorns magazines

Our publishing journey began with a print literary magazine - *redrosethorns magazine 01: community/connection* - followed by two more editions - *redrosethorns magazine 02: home/belonging* and *redrosethorns magazine 03: rebellion/conformity* - in an annual series. Each issue was centred around a theme, reflecting both the growth of our platform and the essential conversations needed to foster positive mental health.

After three years, we decided to complete the series as a trilogy, allowing us to shift our focus toward expanding other publications and creating more events that bring these themes to life.

Thorn & Bloom Magazine

Thorn & Bloom is a quarterly publication exploring self-care as a radical act of resilience and liberation.

Our debut issue, published in March 2025, sparked conversations on socialisation, self-awareness, and critical thinking. The work found within was filled with curated essays, poetry, and reflections on reclaiming autonomy through intentional practice. Because true self-care begins with knowing oneself, and knowing oneself requires confronting the forces that keep us from fulfilment.

Thorn & Bloom

EDITORIAL DIRECTOR

Kirsty Anne Richards

ABOUT THIS MAGAZINE

For our second issue of *Thorn & Bloom Magazine*, we focused on the theme 'Breaking the Cycle', where we present writing that challenges ingrained societal narratives and that interrogate, unravel, and reclaim power over mind, body, and time. Here, words become tools for transformation, offering pathways to freedom through the art of unlearning. Each piece offers insight into how to shatter the constraints that bind us, freeing ourselves to rise into our fullest, most unapologetic being.

LANGUAGE DISCLAIMER

Our publications offer literature from a diverse community found within our global society. To honour the voices of our authors, we have deliberately kept various English dialects found within each persons work and their respective spellings.

ABOUT REDROSETHORNS

redrosethorns is an educational publication company, specialising in literature centred around mental health, self-care, gender & sexuality, and empowerment. Founded on feminist principles, we believe that through art and literature, we can foster empathy and connection to empower each other to live our authentic selves, while building a society that is inclusive and accepting of all diversities.

FROM THE EDITOR

Kirsty Anne Richards is the founder and editorial director of redrosethorns Ltd. Liability Co. (USA) / redrosethorns Ltd. (UK). With a background in psychology, gender/sexuality, and feminism, she is deeply committed to examining the complexities of identity, empowerment, and well-being. Through her work, she strives to create spaces for meaningful dialogue, challenging conventional narratives and encouraging others to cultivate self-worth beyond societal expectations.

An avid reader, Kirsty Anne embraces literature as a vital part of her self-care practice, weaving its lessons into her daily life. She is passionate about the arts and finds joy in travelling, dancing, and writing. She currently lives in London.

Kirsty Anne

EDITORIAL DIRECTOR

Years ago, I heard a story that dragonflies have a one-day lifespan - they are born in the morning, breed during the day, and then die by nightfall. It turns out that this is not true, and it is actually the mayfly that has a 24-hour life cycle. But, regardless of which insect it is, the lesson I took from this remains unchanged: that nothing lasts forever. At the time I heard this, I was also going through one of my darkest moments, and I got a tattoo of a dragonfly on my foot, so that when I felt low, I would look down and be reminded that whatever it was/is I am going through would pass. Now that my facts about the dragonfly have been corrected, I have since learned that they symbolise change, specifically change in the perspective of self-realisation. A transformative figure. So, I guess the meaning of my tattoo remains the same: that change is inevitable, as nothing, no good nor bad, lasts forever.

This understanding reshaped how I approach self-care in profound ways, as it has reinforced my resolve to make necessary changes in my life when something no longer serves me. Psychologically, we tend to cling to familiarity, even when we know it harms us. Breaking out of this cycle can be incredibly painful, which is why we often repeat it despite knowing better. We don't like pain. But the good news is that whatever pain we anticipate through change, it, too, is temporary. And the rewards, though not always immediate, reshape how we engage with life itself.

Thorn & Bloom is rooted in this belief. Prioritising inner care liberates us from patterns in our behaviours that stifle our true selves. To break a cycle, or to make changes in our lives, is not only freeing but an active resistance to suppression, oppression and repression. Personally and politically. We cannot live authentically without dismantling what holds us back, just as we cannot expect a fairer world while upholding the very systems designed to divide and oppress.

Not long after I got that dragonfly tattoo, the personal decisions that followed involved moving to another city, starting a degree, and continuing to get to know the deeper, more hidden parts of myself. I had no connections in said city, nor did I have a home secured. I didn't know how I was going to afford my degree with my slightly-above minimum wage income, and I most certainly never anticipated that getting to know oneself would take a lifetime. But through it all, the one message was clear: if you want something in your life to change, you have to be the one to make the changes, even if you don't know how. The answers come through action. Just as those changes I made in my life magically all worked out.

The greatest reward in learning that change is inevitable - and which brings me closer to my true self - has been the realisation that the capacity to create change lies entirely within me. This is our power. We have the ability to decide what must change, both personally and within society, and we have the capability to take action, sparking a ripple effect that transforms our existence. All social movements are a form of action. All personal growth stems from a decision to take a step. Yes, there will be failure. There will be setbacks. There will also be triumphs. Every emotion will be felt along the way. But through our actions, we generate the shift needed to reshape our lives in ways we can't yet imagine. All we have to do is break the cycle.

"We are a product of our environments, it's true. But at some point in our lives, we become aware of this fact and that awareness presents us with a choice. We get to choose to feel sorry for ourselves and continue on the way we are, or we get to dig deep, figure out exactly why we are the way we are and change it, break the cycle and learn to become the best versions of ourselves."
~ Unknown

Zen Beyond the Bushes

by Juan Schaeren

Rizzy couldn't control himself—or his constant reaction to everything. And that was the underlying issue. The school day ended at three in the afternoon. Most kids lingered in the hallways outside, calling their parents, or participating in after-school activities. Not Rizzy, who sulked all the way to Room 123, escorted by the principal.

"Rizzy, what you did today — throwing those four textbooks on the floor—is unacceptable," the principal said, looking down at him.

He kept walking along the empty corridor. Sweat perspired along the sides of his forehead. "So, what? That only happens once every two weeks. It's not a big deal," he muttered, brushing off his recent actions. The principal sighed, disappointed at Rizzy for not recognizing his mistake. "You need to start managing your emotions. It's an important skill in life."

After a few more steps, they reached the front door of Room 123 — plain white with a silver doorknob. The principal opened the door, creaking as it did. Rizzy followed behind, still remembering the smack that the four textbooks gave off when slammed on the classroom floor. As he stepped in, a thought flickered — him doing things with ease and being happy in the present moment — but it left him as he saw the empty classroom. His eyes quickly turned their attention to a man with a slightly wrinkled face, sitting behind the teacher's desk.

"Wait. Is he going to oversee my detention for today?" asked Rizzy, astonished at seeing the man.

"Yes. This is Coach—,"

"Lao, that I know," interrupted Rizzy.

Rizzy sat on one of the desks, placing his book bag on the floor.

The principal walked over to Coach Lao at the teacher's desk. She gave him a paper. He read it, smirking, giving off a chuckle.

"So, this is the reason why this young boy is in trouble," said Coach Lao in his gentle, assured voice. "Very well, I'll keep a watch on him, and we'll figure out the *root* of the problem."

The principal leaned toward his ear. "He needs to control his emotions. It'll serve him well."

Coach Lao looked to the principal, giving her a look of knowing what he had in front of him. "Okay, he'll benefit while I keep him here."

The principal walked towards the door, looking at Rizzy one more time. "Please behave."

"I'll try," said Rizzy, bothered, his arms crossed.

The door closed, and both Rizzy and Lao sat alone, looking at each other, as the seconds ticked by.

*

Rizzy slouched on the chair, shoulders hunched. The sound of the nearby tree rustled, banging the window with its branches. Coach Lao cleared his throat as he scrolled down his phone. The clock ticked — one, two, three, four, five — another minute passed.

"Well," began Coach Lao, "feel like talking about what happened?"

"I slammed a few books on the floor in class, but that only happens once every few weeks," said Rizzy, his voice shaky. Was he going to yell at him?

"Every few weeks? So, are you going to keep the cycle of slamming every few weeks?" asked Coach Lao, raising his voice in concern.

"I… I overreacted, that's all," spoke Rizzy, his eyes lowering to the side of the desk. Coach Lao leaned back against the chair. His arms were crossed as he thought about Rizzy's response to slamming the books. "Overreacting is an issue that a lot of people nowadays, don't know how to handle. It leads to unnecessary stress, you know? Would you like to stress out unnecessarily?"

Rizzy looked up at the ceiling, in thought, still slouched. "Not really."

"Well, then let's use this detention to rise above it," advised Coach Lao. He stood up from his chair.

Rizzy took out a notebook from his book bag, which Coach Lao looked at with suspicion.

"No, no, no. We're not going to sit here, watching the clock tick," he said. "Your mind needs to be trained on how to let your thoughts pass as if they were clouds. You react because you attach yourself to your own thoughts, instead of letting them go."

Coach Lao walked over to the door. Rizzy kept his eyes staring at him. He opened it and looked back at Rizzy, still sitting down, slouching.

"Well? Let's get going. Pack your things," he said.

Rizzy obeyed, packed the notebook back inside his book bag and rose. They left the classroom behind and walked the empty corridor, hearing the faint sound of laughing children at the front of the school. Then they exited the corridor and walked the outer hallways. The afternoon sun warmed, while the fresh wind breezed through, with the weather being just perfect and not too hot. Up ahead, Rizzy saw the principal and froze. His mind raced. *Uh oh. There's the principal! What'll happen if she sees me with the coach wandering around the hallways?* He felt a knot in his stomach, giving off a huge growl—enough gas for a burp.

"Was that you just now?" asked Coach Lao, looking at him.

"Y-yeah. Sorry about that," replied Rizzy, nervously.

"Alright." There was a brief pause. "Don't worry about her. She'll walk away right… now."

She did. Not noticing them.

*

Coach Lao led Rizzy to a secluded area somewhere off the school grounds. They passed the basketball courts, a pavilion that housed Coach Lao's office, and a soccer field. Rizzy grew concerned about leaving the grounds.

"Coach? Why are we walking off the school hallways and all that," he asked.

Coach Lao stopped ahead of him and turned around. "Ah, you're curious. Good. We're not heading off the grounds completely; instead, I want you to see a place where I go to every morning before the school day begins. It permits me to stay calm throughout the day. We need a calm environment to go to every morning before we lead on with our busy lives."

"Will I be free from my anger once I learn how to train my mind as you said in the classroom?" asked Rizzy.

"Anger is an emotion. It's not that we can train our minds and never get angry again. There are times when anger will present itself, and we have a choice: either succumb to it or learn how to handle it with ease," replied Coach Lao. He turned around and continued walking to the bushes.

A gurgle grew louder. Rizzy heard water flowing, coming from behind the bushes. Coach Lao reached out, burrowing his hand deep into the bushes. He turned to look at Rizzy, who had a sparkle in his eye, curious to see what lay inside.

"Boy, this is the place where I obtain my *zen*," said Coach Lao.

With the might of his arm, Coach Lao swept the bushes aside, revealing the interior — a retreat of some sorts that had beautifully fresh cut grass with a medium-sized fountain perched atop a small hill. On top of the fountain was a Buddha statue with its legs crossed, sitting quietly, letting its mind flow by the constant stream of thoughts. Rizzy entered, stunned by the retreat.

"So, you come here every single morning before the school day begins?" asked Rizzy.

"Yes. This place is a sanctuary for me. My peace comes first. We have to preserve our inner peace since it protects us from the chaos that happens around us," replied the coach.

"Cool," Rizzy replied, though sounding unconvinced by what Coach Lao was getting to.

Coach Lao walked past Rizzy, heading towards the small hill where the fountain was. Rizzy wasn't interested in what Coach Lao was intending him to do here at the retreat, where he got his zen from. It just wasn't ideal for him. He was only thirteen years old with other interests — pranking around with his friends, playing with his smartphone, or trying out sports. Why would he even come close to a retreat where a coach would obtain his zen? Coach Lao stood to the side of the fountain, appreciating the water that flowed out from the top of the Buddha's head as it kept still. He then turned and sat on the cut grass, closing his eyes, taking a breath in and then out before opening them, with Rizzy still at the entrance, gazing at him.

They both glanced at each other. The sparkle that Rizzy had in his eyes was gone. His eyebrows sunk. Coach Lao smiled at him.

"Come here, Rizzy. Here is where the most important part of your detention lies, so let's make the best out of it," he said.

"If you think that I'm sitting there like some monk, then it is a simple no. I'm no monk to begin with," said Rizzy. His anger began rising.

Coach Lao caught the whiff of it and intervened. "There you go. See? You're reacting instead of being open-minded, and that is why you shuffle back into old habits, such as slamming those books onto the ground." There was a pause before Coach Lao continued: "Listen, kid, if you want to make the best out of this detention, then you might as well come sit right next to me and begin the most valuable part of this detention. If not, then you'll stay the same."

A part of Rizzy wanted to run away across the field and into the school, but his instinct was telling him to do as Coach Lao told him: to sit right next to him. He looked both ways, to the retreat and field, with the first choice winning over the second. He walked slowly to the fountain, yet suspicious of what Coach Lao was up to, though trying to ignore his thoughts and let them pass. He sat on the grass, next to the fountain, and looked at what Coach Lao was doing.

"Relax. Breathe in slowly and let it out. If you have any thoughts, then let them pass by like water down a stream. There's no use in attaching to them,"

"Alright, Coach," he said, still with a tone of disinterest. "What is it that we're going to do sitting on the grass?"

Coach Lao opened his eyes. Rizzy was in front of him. He pointed to the small Buddha statue on top of the fountain. "See that statue? Well, that is what you're going to do. Sit still, with your spine aligned straight, and close your eyes."

Rizzy rolled his eyes in disbelief that he was about to do this. He gave a huge sigh. "Whatever this is, it better be useful for the future. If so, then I'll begin using it."

Coach Lao let out a chuckle.

Rizzy crossed his legs and sat up straight. He closed his eyes gently, letting his arms rest on top of his knees. He breathed in, expanding his diaphragm full of air, and let it all out in one big exhale. He followed the practice three times.

"Relax. Breathe in slowly and let it out. If you have any thoughts, then let them pass by like water down a stream. There's no use in attaching to them," said Coach Lao, calmly, keeping his eyes closed. The next ten minutes were spent in quietude. The water spurted out from the top of the Buddha's head and gurgled into the base of the fountain. The breeze blew by with Rizzy inhaling the fresh, clean quality of it into his lungs, exhaling out the unwanted stress. His head bobbed at times, prompting him to almost fall asleep. At times, Rizzy would hear his mind chatter — *Slam those books on the ground again. Why are you even sitting down on the grass? It is not for you. Be angry.* But he would ease himself, not listening to them, and letting the thoughts pass. Suddenly, he heard a gentle clap two times. He woke up and found Coach Lao sitting, looking at him.

"So, you feel any different?" he asked.

Rizzy had his eyes a bit wide, sensing a calm aura around him. He remembered being in turmoil hours ago of slamming a book on the ground, then reacting at the coach's guidelines for detention, but something felt different. He looked at the palms of his hands and thought to himself, *I feel different. Calm to be exact.*

"Calm," replied Rizzy.

Coach Lao both nodded and gave him a smile "That's it. What we just did, sitting still in a calm environment, is called meditation. People meditate to seek inner peace, a sense of calmness within oneself, but most importantly, for knowledge on how to transcend our traumas and insecurities."

An alarm went off suddenly, catching them both off guard. It was coming from Coach Lao's watch. "Ah, time's up. We've finished for today, Rizzy. Detention is finally over." He turned it off.

Detention was over, but the lesson was far from it. Rizzy got up from the grass with the help of Coach Lao, who gave him a hand. They both made their way to the entrance of the retreat, exiting it and continuing with their lives. For Rizzy, it was the beginning of a new journey to everlasting peace with himself and to transcend into a better version of himself through meditation.

***

Rewilding
by Kara Dorris

In hunger, sweetgrass-eating mouths & suffocating hooves. By which I mean this is not an excuse. You love lemon drops, suckle the sweet & spit out the sour. Onions make you puke, uneasy around anything more layered than you. You flinch around Jello, around anything as easy to cut through as skin. Not being able to tease out nutmeg in pumpkin bread makes you afraid, as if you'll get lost in the folds of another. Not knowing where your meat comes from makes you imagine slaughterhouses & baby unicorns; the baby chickens your aunt used to raise. The ones inside the greenhouse so full it was like yellow shag carpet. The ones you'd chase, run with. The ones you never realized, until years later, were terrified of you. In terror, we hunted wolves almost to extinction, but you've read about rewilding, how those wolves help forests grow. You know we must bring them back—despite teeth & claws & learned fears.

"Not everything that is faced can be changed, but nothing can be changed until it is faced."
~ James Baldwin

Palimpsest: Written in Scars
by Serenella Velez

Palimpsest *noun*
/ˈpaləm(p)ˌsest/

1. a manuscript or piece of writing material on which the original writing has been effaced to make room for later writing, but of which traces remain.

Subject Classification: Homo sapiens, XX chromosomal pattern (approx. age: coming)

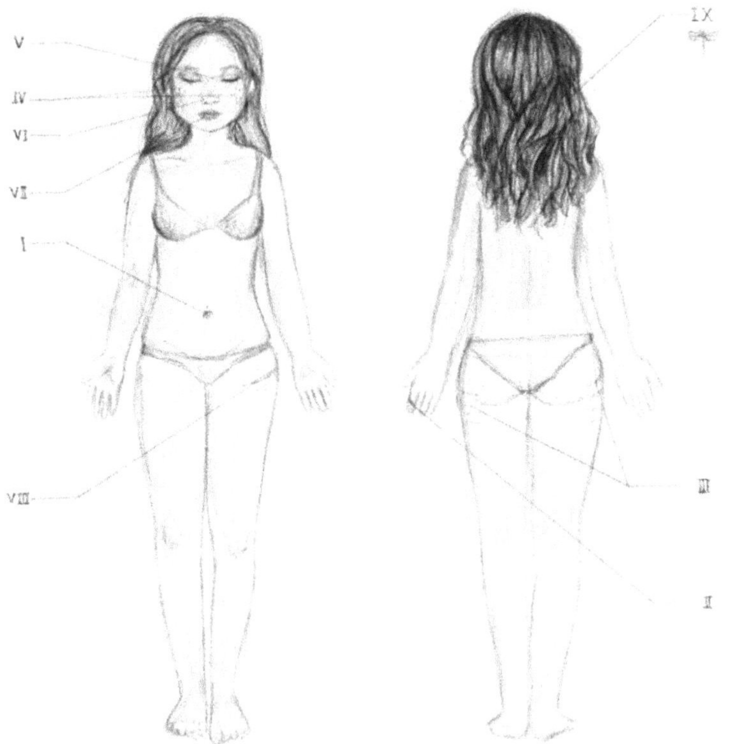

Figure 1: Outer

I. Navel

A. You were born with a scar. Not the bloody kind, not the kind anyone weeps over. A quiet wound, tied off and dismissed. A neat little knot of tissue where connection used to be. They coo its name at you, something sweet, almost ridiculous: belly button. As if it's not the first time the world told you: *you are alone now*. This is where the story begins, not in breath or voice, but in severance. A canvas was born the moment the cord was cut.

II. Index Finger

A. She was laughing when it happened. A snip of metal, a slip, and the world bloomed red across your skin. Your blood soaked through construction paper, staining your seventh-grade art project. She cried harder than you did, burying her face in your shoulder, as if her guilt needed more comforting than your pain. You didn't ask to be the one bleeding. But you learned to hold others anyway. Not everyone who hurts you knows how to hold what they've broken.

III. Thigh (1)

A. The lines came quietly, like whispers. Was it puberty? Aging? The way sadness thickened solid beneath your skin? Regardless, you learned early how to drape fabric over the record of becoming. Your boyfriend swears he doesn't see them. *But you do.*

IV. Cheeks

A. You waged war against your reflection. Benzoyl peroxide, salicylic acid, cleanse, conceal, erase, conceal again. Some days, you felt more foundation than flesh. The blemishes became punctuation in sentences you never meant to write. Each layer was a revision. Each swipe, a word crossed out. But the red bled through the page.

V. Nasal bridge

A. There was a boot, a blur, and then metal met bone. You were front row, center of the universe, when the universe presented pain as a gift. The band saw you. Security fetched you a Band-Aid. For a moment, the singer was God, you the chosen one. They offered you a half-empty water bottle like communion, handed you the setlist like scripture. You bled under the lights. The scar has mostly faded. But part of you wishes it wouldn't. You don't get many chances to say: *here's proof that something unforgettable happened to me.*

VI. Nose (piercing)

A. In the quiet of your own room, you sat before the mirror. The needle was sharp, but your resolve was sharper. It wasn't pain you feared; it was the lack of it. You wanted to feel it, wanted proof that you could bear it, endure it. So, you pierced your own skin, a small rebellion against your own softness. The blood was warm, like defiance in its purest form. You didn't ask for permission; you didn't need it. It was yours to claim. Now, you have a gold stud to show for it.

VII. Lips

A. You once bled before a thousand people. Now, you bleed in front of no one. Teeth catch skin. A flick, a tear. You chew through nerves like paper. Exams. Waiting rooms. The hush before you say a thing you can't take back. When asked about your peeling lips, you say it must be the dry weather. You're from Louisiana.

VIII. Thigh (2)

A. No matter how fast blood runs its course, it will never unsee the light of day. Healing is not forgetting. The body remembers its edits. Every line struck through; every revision etched in scar tissue. The blood dries. The weight lingers.

IX. Nape (tattoo)

A. There comes a moment when you've had enough, when the story carved into your skin no longer feels like yours. So, you take the pen. Beneath the veil of your hair, you inscribe a soft defiance: a dragonfly, *Libélula*, your name as your father once sang it. Etched where only tenderness dares to look, it waits beneath the brush of an intimate hand. A secret rebellion. A reclamation. At last, the pen was held not by the world, but by you.

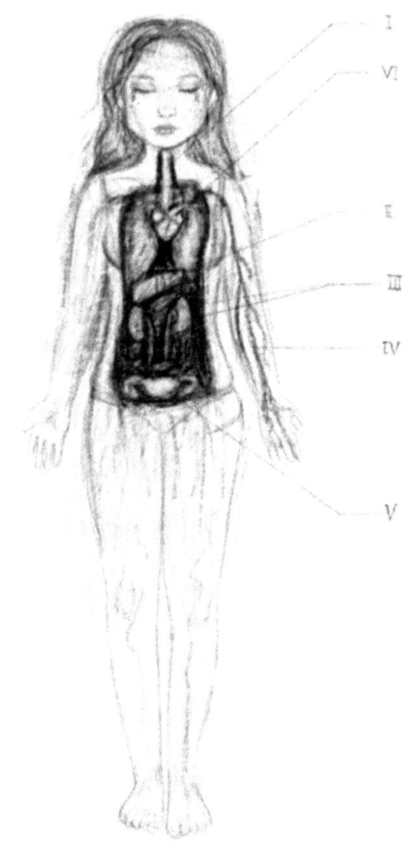

Figure 2: Inner

I. Esophagus

A. Burned from the inside out. There's no poetry in bile. Still, your throat carries the echo of every refusal. Of everything that wouldn't stay down. You keep the burn like a buried scream. Some pain asks not to be seen. Some stories aren't written on the skin but swallowed.

II. Liver

A. Your party days, when recklessness clung to you like perfume. Every bad decision sugar-slick on your tongue, intoxicating, indulgent, freedom. But when left out too long, freedom turns bitter.

III. Kidneys

A. How many times can you purify yourself before the blood becomes too tired to run clean? You've lived on the edge of your own expectations, rinsing away mistakes like they're just stains on a tablecloth. But even your kidneys know: it's never enough. It's a cycle that never reaches the core, a cleansing that's only skin deep. You keep filtering the poisons, scrubbing the damage, and yet there's always more. The body asks, demands, gives, and still, *it's never enough.*

IV. Blood

A. The great archivist. It carries every version of you: child, lover, liar, survivor. It remembers what you've tried to forget, holds what you've tried to shed. It runs its cycle, steady and unyielding, filtering the toxins you let in. You may believe there are moments of purity, but there aren't. You can transfuse the body, but never deceive the bloodstream.

V. Womb

A. Erasing and rewriting over and over, until the paper tears. They tell you your body will be ruined, too many scars, too many stretch marks, skin spilling over, fat softening the edges. They say the canvas will be torn, that you will be nothing but fragments, a sacrifice to the labor of life. They tell you, you won't heal this time, what is done can't be undone. But you know something they don't: healing doesn't erase. Healing rewrites. The marks are chapters, each one telling a story, each line making room for the next. You are not torn; you are a canvas that expands, writing the story of a body that gives life without ever losing its own. The paper may tear, but the story goes on.

VI. Heart

A. Pumping your blood, it holds the weight of what you've seen. It bruised when they hurt you, when they left you. You keep calling it soft, but softness is not weakness. You see, it never stopped beating. Not through grief. Not through shame. It beats despite the weight; despite the versions of love you've had to outgrow. You can't erase the scars caused by what it's held. But you can teach it a new rhythm. You're still here.

And that's revision worth keeping.

***

No Son of That Silence

by Agbeye Oburumu

A strong man, they said, buries his heart in iron.
And at seven, I was taught to walk on nails—and stand still.
No tears, they said, just duty.
I packed my boyhood in brass suitcases,
keeping down the fire of curiosity with frigid submission.
In class, I folded silent paper boats
and helped them swim across the lake of words I wanted to hold back.
Sleep was a room with no windows,
my voice a sparrow trapped inside a hollowed chest.
And they taught me how to be a soldier of silence. Today I stand taller, I unlearn the hymns of the old obedience.
My palms are cupped, full of the morning's first light.
I Protest with Every Breath I Take:
a material of tenderness flowering out of ashes.
I turn my face to the sun and weep as though weeping is rain,
to wash away the dust of "be a man."
I look in the mirror, and there is a stranger—
a tender riot of muscle and memory.
I do not water The roots of gentleness.
with storming rivers of rage.
I fight with softness, I defend with vulnerability. I reclaim every lost prayer,
lulling my own soul to sleep.
and when I dance alone in the dark, it's not shame,
but defiance in each step.
The boy in me is fire; the man understands by now.
how to burn brilliantly, without incinerating himself.

Miscellaneous Junk
by Cassie McCay

Say I were to unfold
all the parts of me
that hold me back
    lay them out
    on the table
    have a good look at them
would I find some junk
from 20 years ago
that I picked up
& never put down
because I thought
surely, I might need it someday?
Perhaps notions about my capability-
    a rusty hacksaw
    for cutting into my self-efficacy
wariness of my own gender
of femininity-
    an old pendant I wore
    for warding off confusing danger
    itchy disconnects
a deep quest for good enough
lovable enough-
    a gnawing ice-cream scoop
    overused for scraping up
    a myriad of things
      love
      desire
    & piling them into a cavern inside
where I should instead be looking
to marvel at all the stalagmites
that reside.

The Unspoken

by Grace Flaherty

I. The First Warning

Catherine dated my Uncle Rich for a while before they got married, and even as an eight-year-old, I thought she was too beautiful for him. She had long bleach-blonde hair that fell in careful waves and a smile so bright it almost made you squint. Against her warm, sunlit complexion, she looked like someone who belonged in a movie, not at the dining table of my grandmother's house.

I adored her immediately. Until then, the only women around on that side of the family were my grandmother and my mom, who must have noticed the way I gravitated toward Catherine, like a moth to a lamp.

"So, Catherine," my mom said one night, her voice lilting with a teasing edge, "Grace is starting to play softball this spring for the first time."

She nudged my elbow hard. I nudged her back, grinning, eager for Catherine's approval.

"Oh, wow..." Catherine said, drawing out the word with mock surprise. She flipped her hair over one shoulder, eyes glinting. "Is she batting for the other team while she's at it?"

She tossed her hands in the air and laughed — a sound as bright as her smile. I don't know if the whole room froze, but my mom did.

"Excuse me?"

"Oh, you know — softball, lesbians? Just never mind," Catherine said, still laughing, as if she hadn't cracked something open.

"No, I don't know," my mother snapped, whisking her glass of red wine into the other room.

I trailed after her, my sneakers squeaking on the linoleum floor. I remember asking what Catherine had meant. I don't remember exactly how my mother answered. What I do remember is the tension, how it hung in the air—heavy, metallic—and how the night never quite recovered.

That moment calcified inside me: an unspoken warning about what certain kinds of love might cost.

Catherine married Uncle Rich not long after, but a few years later, she cheated on him during a trip they booked together to Los Angeles. It was a betrayal the family never entirely forgave, though it was often referenced in the same half-laughing tone as her own earlier comment. Almost as if cruelty, when wrapped in enough beauty, could somehow be excused.

II. Lies We Tell Ourselves

By the time I was twelve, that warning had grown roots inside me.

Two girls in my orchestra class started dating, and the whole room rippled with whispers and giggles, as if Chloe and Lexi's relationship gave everyone else permission to publicly audit their private beliefs about love.

"Chloe and Lexi?!" Maya gasped, her mouth wide open.

"No way," Ella said, laughing. She had just come out herself. Bold and shaky, her voice was still uncertain but growing stronger every day. "I love when a queer couple pops out of nowhere."

"Me too," Lizzy said. "I saw it coming since Mrs. McPeck's second-period science."

It was Maya who turned the conversation serious. "Are you guys also gay? Because I genuinely don't know myself. I accept all and I'm curious but...I'm not sure if it's for me."

There was a pause.

"I'm not gay," I blurted out, too fast, too loud. "I would never treat anyone differently because of that lifestyle," I added, my voice tripping over itself to sound progressive, "but it's not for me. I'm happy for Chloe and Lexi, though."

Even as I said it, a thin shame coiled inside me. I wasn't lying exactly. I wasn't gay, I told myself. I wasn't anything. I was just twelve.

Molly nodded slowly. "I'm not sure what I am," she said, "but I agree about the acceptance part."

We shuffled our sheet music and forced some jokes, pretending it didn't matter.

But it mattered to me. I thought about it all the way home, and for many years after that.

III. Laughter as Armor

As I got older, the silences around me became louder.

When one of my aunts died young, we gathered in my Uncle Charlie's Dorchester townhouse to drink and grieve in the only way my big Irish Catholic family knew how: by trying to laugh louder than the sadness.

The house smelled of beer and cold cuts, wood paneling sweating from the press of bodies.

"I remember the first time my father met Gumby," Uncle Jeff said, hoisting his beer like a trophy.

Gumby, whose real name I never knew, had grown up with my dad. He was short and stocky with a soft face—like Sean Astin in *Rudy*, if he'd never touched a football.

"That fucker strolled in and said he was studying to be a nurse," Uncle Jeff said, roaring. "And my father, God rest his soul, looks at him, looks at me, then back at him and goes, 'What are you, a fucking faggot?'"

The crowd erupted. Laughter rang off the yellowed ceiling tiles.

I laughed too. Not because it was funny, but because the sound was tidal, irresistible. Because not laughing would have meant standing alone.

IV. Grief Ignored

Auntie Katie wore her signature *Life is Good* t-shirts, loose over her stocky frame, and kept her hair in a neat men's crew cut. Her hot pink nail polish was the only small rebellion against an otherwise practical life. She lived with her "best friend," Deidre, for twenty-five years in a tiny Boston apartment.

No man was ever mentioned. No husband, no ex-boyfriend, no whispers of heartbreak. Just Deidre, whose appearances at family gatherings grew rarer as I grew older. As if she knew her presence could only be tolerated if it stayed unexplained.

When Katie died, Deidre and their circle of friends packed up all her belongings into boxes and left them silently on the stoop of the Flaherty family home. No condolences. No hugs. Just cardboard tombs and silence.

“There comes a moment when you’ve had enough, when the story carved into your skin no longer feels like yours. So, you take the pen. Beneath the veil of your hair, you inscribe a soft defiance: a dragonfly, Libélula, your name as your father once sang it.”
~ Serenella Velez

My other aunts were furious. They blacklisted
Deidre and her friends like excommunicated parishioners. As we drank and wept and remembered Katie, I heard it in their voices. The anger, the confusion, the betrayal. *How dare they, after everything?*

It took me years to understand: Deidre hadn't abandoned us.

We had abandoned her, long before Katie died. Deidre was a widow. A real one. But to acknowledge that would have meant acknowledging a life some of us were too afraid to see.

Maybe Katie included.

V. Naming It

Sometimes now, I linger at family gatherings, a glass of wine in my hand, my mouth half-open, waiting. Waiting for someone to say it. Waiting for someone to acknowledge that the "friend" I've started "hanging around" with—the girl with the fiery red hair and opal eyes—isn't my "roommate," isn't my "buddy," isn't "like a sister."

She's my girlfriend. She's Katie. Katherine.

It's funny how this story started with a Catherine, twisted itself around a Katie, and now ends with someone of my own, who goes by both.

Internalized homophobia, I've learned, is a slow poison. It seeps into the cracks between love and language until even your own mouth forgets how to name the thing you cherish most. Overcoming it doesn't mean the world around you changes; it only means you stop letting their silence be yours too.

Maybe someday they'll see us. Maybe they won't.

But when she slips her hand into mine under the table at these gatherings, I hold it tight. And for once, I don't look away.

***

The Disappointed Optimist

by Larry Kilman

Doing the same thing over and over again
expecting different results is a definition of insanity
often attributed to Einstein, a wise saying even if it wasn't his.

Yet I do this in painful relationships, finding echoes of the past
in the present. Even using the same words,
awareness dawning as I spiral into familiar scenarios.

I know it is healthy to break toxic behavior,
to wean myself off the comfort of habit,
to understand I make bad choices. It is the first step to betterment.

So why is it so difficult to stop choosing inappropriately,
to find what is nigh impossible, the most appealing?

There is something to be said about forgetting the last fight,
to let it slide, the words too awful and unfair.
Better to bury it, hope for the best and start again.

Besides, people change, of course they do,
if you give them a chance to rise to it
rather than hold them to lower expectations,

careful not to bail too quickly,
maintaining a fine balance requiring patience
and a willful suspension of disbelief,

until I am once again in well-known territory,
our words grappling like there are no tomorrows,
a collection of non-sequiturs because we talk in circles.

This closed loop is maddening and instinctive,
a return to the chagrin of discordance.
This time, I promise, for the last time.

Bubblegum Yoga Outfit Is Coming Soon

by CJ The Tall Poet

For my ideal bubblegum yoga outfit
I will choose to develop a short black afro
My voice must showcase vast innocence
Rather than pointless aggression
A simple screaming oak tree scent
Was replaced by something fruity and bright
Some shivers started from uncomfortable truths
The chest pain seems to be messaging me
It shall strengthen the creativity I use

Someday I'll Love Neecie

by Denise Buitre

After Ocean Vuong
After Frank O'Hara / After Roger Reeves

Neecie, don't self-sabotage. Not again, they say there is a light at the end of the tunnel but the darkness swallows it whole, and it is here that you are held. Dark needn't mean evil and is not equivalent to bad. Antithesis to light, but Neecie, sometimes the brightness is blinding. Here's the bed you lay in alone, but to be alone implies loneliness, and you cannot abide by that. Let your eyes adjust and you will see the shapes unfold before you, familiarize your eyes and see that yang is as integral as the moon. Tides rise and your thighs fall apart as easily as your heart. Annessa says, if you put the rhyme in, it will bury itself deep. Don't self-sabotage, never again. Cycles are meant to be broken, before you bury yourself in your sorrow, Neecie. I swear, you will love yourself enough to call yourself Denise.

“Besides, people change, of course they do,
if you give them a chance to rise to it
rather than hold them to lower expectations,”
~ Larry Kilman

A Conversation with Rachel Lorraine

interviewed by Kirsty Anne Richards

Rachel Lorraine is a Self-formed, multi-expressional Artist. A creative alchemist in language and visuals, her work calls forth the cerebral and visceral to shape shift memory and lens through emotional expression. Uniting poetry, oil painting and Self portrait photography in themes that aim to illuminate the dark, taped off alleyways of the human condition, consciousness and conditioning; luring light towards awareness, Self reflection, Self knowledge/exploration, embodiment, reclamation, healing, evolution...revolution.

Kirsty Anne Richards: I adore your art. It is powerful, empowering, and very sensual. You are so brave to show yourself and your art so daringly bold. I admire the insightfulness each image holds. And it inspires me to reflect within myself, so that I, too, can show up more of my whole self. Unapologetically.

Rachel Lorraine: First of all, may I start by saying a deep thank you for this conversation and expressing to me how you experience my work! What you feel and take from it and apply to Self is exactly what I embody and hope to create for others within what I do; it is not just the work itself but the mirror I hope to reflect back to one's soul - the invitation, to See beyond the societal veil and excavate what we are taught to fear - Ourselves.

K: Thank you, and I must say, art is powerful in that sense: it provides society with a reflection of themselves, where the power lies in not what makes us feel good, but what makes us face the shadow parts of ourselves. I'm curious to know what sparked your desire to start creating art?

R: Art was always my chosen form of communication and expression since birth. It was never something I would just do, as one would a hobby or distraction. It was born to me, like an appendage, a limb...never something I could detach or think of as separate or learned part of my being; instantly guttural, intuitive and healing. Out of the womb, I demanded paper and crayons. It was how I made sense of the world around me when words didn't exist to reflect my reality, and emotions too flooded to verbalize. That's something I fully realize now, looking back to form words to it - as a baby, all through youth till now, magnetized to art supplies and a quiet corner to spill it all out of me, it was instinct, natural drive to form such feelings into focus and to find safety. A sacred place within me allowed out.

K: How would you describe your artistic voice to someone encountering your work for the first time?

R: My artistic voice...to use this language literally in imagery, what I hear is something that is designed to echo, reflecting thought amidst abandoned or blocked off cavernous walls...its tonality and vibration once silenced, now unleashed to quake and crumble the conditioned narratives that built these ominous structures that trap us in. Its pitch, a warm drone hums not to merely tremble surface waters, but awaken the depths neglected and unexplored. I dive first - to show you the water is safe, for how can I ask you to go where I myself refuse? My work bears a light, a candle I carry into the dark, for it is in the dark, that we find Ourselves. My artistry is a love letter to Self knowing, Self discovery, healing, embodiment and personal evolution.

K: Amazing! And a poignant reminder that we find ourselves looking in, and I also think in looking back at ourselves, as we can find clues of what influenced our beings. Were there any early influences or experiences that shaped who you are today?

R: There are many experiences that shaped me into the form I stand in today. I mean, we all come from a rich life of many wonderful and horrible things. All of which influence our psyche, our actions, relationships, how we connect - to Self and others, in turn, our expressions. Trauma gives you pathways - it is one's choice to either sit with the harm and let it chain and distort you, which affects every facet of one's life, brain and body in present

Image on the left:
Gravity
by Rachel Lorraine

Photography.

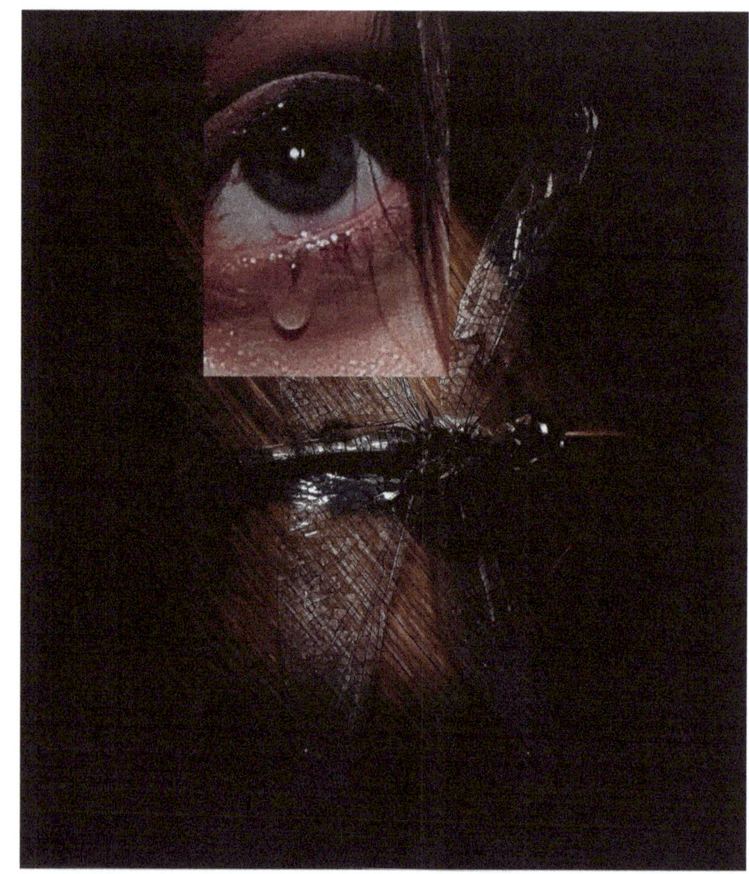

Image on the right:
Wings of Freyja
by Rachel Lorraine

Photography.

and future - or one can choose to transmute it and claim a personal path to healing. In choosing the latter, it has taken me on many unexpected turns personally and artistically, as my work is my chosen alchemy in this venture. It frees me from the conditioned Self and introduces me to who I Am. I awaken deeper with each piece. Nothing is more healing than embodying one's true Self that was never allowed to be. We have the power in each of us to find our own freedom; it begins first with choice, courage and excavation.

K: Can you share a belief or behaviour you were taught growing up that you've since had to unlearn?

R: Unlearning is the most vital action we can take to reclaim ourselves; I firmly believe. We are so heavily conditioned. I have had to unlearn, and still am - I believe we forever are - most things I have had magnetized to me, through direct or indirect teachings in relation to life, how I view the world and myself, which of course affects my output, personally and artistically. I believe one of the most important things to unlearn for us All is the imposed narrative of perfectionism. I never understood it, in fact, found its "results" unappealing, empty, thin. For one, it's imaginary, a bias, individualized illusion, and so much power should not be given to a ghost designed to haunt and taunt you. It is the fastest 'why' to disconnect from Self. As a creative soul, nothing is more harmful and severing from source. As a human being, nothing more debilitating. If grown in environments that praise the concept and claim its identity with pride, blind to its mental/ emotional toxin and the dead art it breeds, you lose yourself before you begin, and you fight your whole life to find You in another's belief. Erase this one. Delete the concept - invisible weight placed upon your

chest cannot resuscitate you or better your output - in fact, it harms it. Find your freedom, begin with the delete button. This one's a good place to start.

K: I could not agree more. It's what bores me to tears on social media nowadays. The constant copying and trying to fit an ideal that does not exist in reality. Making things look perfect takes away the humanity, the beautiful messiness that makes us unique. I am trying to embrace the more natural side of me, too, because I know deep down that that is where I will thrive, whatever that may look like. Tell me, was there a moment when you realised, *This doesn't belong to me, this was taught to me?* What sparked that awareness?

R: Shame. We are handed down shame like a precious family heirloom, a tattered dress worn to threads, so fragile everyone fears to pick it up but cannot throw away, for to acknowledge it, is to hold it close...and it will fall apart and get messy - no one wants to feel too deeply, so it's passed around instead. Fear runs the show - look closely and you will see it is at the root of most things. Shame its leader. There have been many moments shame was handed to me, and I knew it wasn't mine to hold. But I had to question - everything. That knowledge and awareness doesn't subside the pain, but it activates the process of healing. You must always follow the threads to its origins to discover what is truly yours to carry. A shareable example is when I evolved to utilize my body more fluidly in my work, as part of the story, the vessel, the creator, as the Art it is, the storyteller, shown as a unifying element - because spoiler alert! we all have a body - I noticed discomfort, jokes and unsupportive commentary from those who have projected their relationship with their own bodies onto me - and/or their ownership of their concept of me; of which revealing I do have a Women's body I claim as my own, paired with the "sudden" emergence of Voice...dashed it somehow. I couldn't fit the role I was assigned any longer. I outgrew the box I was planted in within those minds, forgetting I am not an artificial plant, and roots are born to expand. How blasphemous! What a disappointment to show embodiment...How fragile we are, huh?

K: I experienced something similar when I, too, started showing my body more confidently and sensually. Oh, how others criticised and gasped at the audacity I had to express myself outside the 'rules' I was meant to abide. I found it so old-fashioned, so petty, that my body had sent others up in arms. After all, it is mine to do with as I will. Following on this, how do you navigate the tension between who you truly are and who you were conditioned to be?

R: The tensions of who I Am vs. who I was conditioned to be are always an awareness and driving force in my expressions, healing and daily life - it demands me to put my foot to the gas pedal and push through to my true existence and experience; to challenge those shadows. I shed my skin continuously, I do it openly, I do it unapologetically, I do it afraid. I do it because I must have air, and who I was conditioned to be was formed in a box without oxygen. So now I breathe - I CREATE the oxygen as a reminder that who I Am has the right to exist, as I Am and who I will become is also welcome. And who I was? merely a ghost of other people's desires and projections of which there was no room for us all to exist safely... so I chose myself. I choose myself daily, in compassion and continued curiosity. I let my personal process be seen, to evaporate the narrative of what we "should" be, and instead embody who We Are in this moment As we are. It's a journey, as we are always meant to grow and evolve, moving ever closer to our personal truth, of which can also evolve. A truth I crave to know deeper. I wrote a poem on this entitled - A Roar Silenced Still Must Sound.

K: I love that! 'A Roar Silenced Still Must Sound.' Have you ever had parts of your art or story that were once silenced or softened for the comfort of others?

R: I've dimmed my light and muted my sound all my years in agreement to the illusions of safety, love, acceptance, and to create comfort and protection for others. I learned early, unchallenging and unthreatening = safe. What I observed, absorbed and experienced. But the rift that is created internally by imposed or chosen silence and "performing" can be more agonizing and creates literal dis-ease and conditions in the physical body. To exist in unauthentic forms and compromised dualities rattles your center, as your core of being is screaming to wake you up and silence the fear you learned before it calcifies into illness and destruction; begging you to get to the other side, because it knows you can, that you are strong enough and safe enough to do it. Your body communicates and tells you when you are out of alignment - we must learn to listen. But we are magnetic, malleable and absorbent creatures, which can be a positive if utilized for growth, but also a negative if not...we become sheep - afraid of our own minds and the rest of the herd...and fear breeds hate. What we allow in shapes our internal world, which then shapes our output. Also, we are regretfully assigned roles in our relationships since birth and all through life; some you never meant to take on or didn't know you agreed to...the terms with fine print so small you neglected its presence, until one day you realize you lost your voice entirely to the outside world, reciting a script written for you - and you aren't even sure what your Own voice sounds like to Yourself. Once deeply discovered, I made it my personal mission to patiently and lovingly peel back the layers I kept for warmth and survival. To use my unique voice in honesty, no matter how it was conditioned to tremble, and the laughter that ensues from its cracking and stutter. I let it all be seen, for No one is meant to stay hidden, and our humanity is not meant to be disguised. Those who champion embodiment often shame ones who do when they witness it actually being done. Do it anyway. Make noise - so you can Hear Yourself.

K: I watched this show once where someone said, 'Secrets make you sick,' and something shifted inside me. A deep knowing that I had to release, or I would get sick. And now I feel so uncomfortable when I can't be myself, like I must purge, leave, change something, or I will get sick being still and stagnant. The one thing I want to scream from the rooftops is to tell others to get to know themselves. Know your body, know your needs and desires, get to know your thoughts, trauma and triggers, and what lights up your soul, because once you do, you will naturally honour the being you are. You will be less susceptible to societal conditioning, and that is what self-care is all about. Finding you and standing tall in your most authentic self. It is the greatest gift you can offer others. I'm interested to know, what does self-care look like to you? Or can you share a self-care practice that has helped your growth?

R: To me, pockets of alone time to self-connect, reflect, play and explore are very vital for my functionality and happiness. It grounds me and lets my inner child roam freely. Visiting with myself routinely in my own personal world keeps me balanced, clear and connected - replenishes me and rejuvenates. Also, the words we choose to repeat outwardly and internally hold great power-creative energy, that train and structure our minds, which manifest its beliefs - we are Creators. So, being aware of the language I use daily, with Self and others, has reshaped my experience in life for the better. Everything becomes lighter and more aligned. I find this awareness to be a great act of Self care, ownership and loving foresight for Self. We create the world we speak into existence, so choose wisely with intention. For example, remove the word "try" from your vocabulary and see what happens. You will mess up a lot at first, catch it and keep going. Seems innocent enough, but you get what you ask for, so to try is to never arrive, right? Do or do not, action and reaction - there is no in between, literally it's what is. Turns out a simple, common word such as this holds the energetic power to keep us stagnant. By changing your words, you shift your perspective, creating a new environment. Speaking kindly to yourself is a healing act and spreads forward to others. We are more powerful than we want to believe.

...cont. on page 58

Image above:
Am I Painting, Am I Woman, Am I Chair?
by Rachel Lorraine

Oil painting/ Self portrait.

Exorcism of Perfect

by Rita Moe

—after Roseann Lloyd

Good, better, best. Never let it rest.
'Til your good is better and your better best.
—St. Jerome (c. 342–347 – 420)

Good, with a capital G,
you're wearing me out:
Better Perform; be Best-in-Class.
I tell you now: I decline.
Never and Always, Shoulds and Shalt Nots:
let those bossy bovines out to pasture.
It pleases me to decide for myself
when to rest, when to drive through
'til morning.
No thank you
to judgment and rankings.
Good-bye to constant striving.
Is a straight, fast freeway
better than a winding, dusty road?
And mile markers—
your holy goal posts—
serve no better purpose
than do best-laid plans to the prairie sky.

Black Boy
by Thomas Beckwith

Black boy, Black boy, you used
to have so much joy.
Black boy you used to dance,
laugh, read, and spell out loud.
Black boy what happened?
You were never coy. Black
boy, Black boy, what
happened to your joy?
Black boy, Black boy, we
see you. Black boy, just be
you! Black boy, Black boy,
you're not bad. Black boy,
Black boy, we hear you.
Black boy, Black boy, do
you need a hug? Black boy,
Black boy, you're not a
thug.
Black boy, you're loved.
Black boy, hold your head up high.
Black boy, Black boy,
there is no need to lie.
Black boy, it's okay to cry.
Black boy, we want to hug you.
Black boy, Black boy, don't let
people steal your joy. Black boy,
Black boy, don't let their words
destroy you. Black boy, Black
boy, the world needs your joy.
Black boy, here's a hug. Black boy,
Black boy, we love you!

Body Language
by Melanie White-Heron

When I was forty, I understood my mother and father brought the war across the ocean and handed it down through their bodies. At eighteen, my father enlisted in the Royal Navy, served on a minesweeper stationed in the Mediterranean, was sprayed down with DDT, triggering a protracted battle against the landmine of skin cancer. He spent much of his life steering clear of disruption, always avoiding, infrequently docking, never really resting comfortably against the shore of another. His hull of a body, reliable and predictable, and mostly impenetrable; his exterior, mostly calm, a remote greyish khaki was camouflage. While he avoided bombs, my mother needed to set them off, a reminder she was no longer evacuated far from home; she survived. The fumes of war smoldered at the edges of my childhood and lodged in the core of my movements. My mother feared lung cancer, while other forms of unrest replicated inside. My father feared emotional connections, feelings and bonds, which in forming demand the revelation of an inner self. Illnesses of the mind and the flesh formed my first language.

When I was thirty, my father moved in with us in a literal sense, though not really. He'd sit quietly reading the newspaper, leaving for months at a time, riding his bike across different countries. We'd see him leaving, then returning, always moving. Even stationary, he was miles away. He never said so, but I think my father's motion kept him safe. Consumed with sustaining the form, he countered change, repelled aging, denied disease, which was a question of will, a moral failing. A body trained to keep eyes forward, not looking back, and not looking here, now at the ground beneath his feet. He resisted rest, which invites reflection; a terrible thing if one fears an emotional life, so he kept his body in motion. The war made him a sailor. The war made him an emigrant. After war, can anyone really return home to rest?

When I was twenty-four, I left the destruction of one home and created another: I moved and married. With restlessness by my side and discomfort in my body, my first husband suggested running, and I decided on marathons, thinking I could force my grandmother's hips into an acceptable size. My mother called to tell me that he was a "Svengali." She didn't see the irony while he didn't understand the slight. But he did understand that desirable wives are thin and not selfish, that running serves an aesthetic purpose. Finding or being or understanding my own body contributed nothing. And still, I feared some misinterpretation hidden inside. So, I followed my mother's lead and left him.

With my parent's battle beneath my skin, I kept running, a bodily rebellion in every foot falling against the unnatural concrete. I bought a necklace with 26.2 on the hanging pendant and wore it religiously, thinking this devotional struggle would provide comfort. Until the cheap metal alloy tarnished, staining the skin above my heart while I failed to recognize the metaphor. Early morning runs grated against nature, each stride demanding, pushing, scolding my body to vanish along empty suburban sidewalks. I practiced conformity in each run, and once I had completed a marathon, I'd eat fries from a chip truck, telling myself that I deserved them, that I had earned them. And I ignored the growing ache in my left hip.

When I was eighteen, my father demanded a degree, so I moved into residence at the University of Guelph and started smoking. Not out of some rebellious streak. Instead, I inhaled as a sort of benign assimilation into scene and circumstance, a way of breathing, a movement I'd learned. I joined friends whose svelte bodies moved next to mine, wanting to look like them, to shrink my hips, and to quell my appetite. As a literature student, I wanted to craft my own manuscript of a dangerous life, unaware of the pantomime. Coffee and cigarettes were still cool back then. Food was optional, indulgent. Fat was imperfect, evidence of flawed character in the minds of working-class parents born amidst air raids and rationing. They wanted a peaceful life with children who complied.

When I was seventeen, my mother sighed and I heard her whisper, "Oh dear," then watched her head drop with the realization that I had inherited my grandmother's hips. I decided to forego breakfast and lunch, leaving only enough time in the day for dinner. Praise and attention were rewards for a body disappearing. My father has a Polaroid photo of me in *The Year of Great Deprivation* on a suburban basement sofa, all outdated browns and beiges of the 1970s. I remember this scene – at the end of a school day, I had just come home, fallen forward, passed out, face down like a sideways semicolon. My father wordlessly snapped this photo, pleased with this version of his daughter's body. The photo froze a moment, unchanging other than the gentle fading of earthy hues, a form of devotion in capturing me unaware.

"When my body began to speak its own language, I had to listen. Language requires a speaker and a listener, a writer and a reader. I felt that mindless movement and compliance are like cancer cells growing restlessly."

When I was fifteen, my mother packed up, left my father, my brother and me in the suburbs and moved downtown. Considered beautiful in the way of Elizabeth Taylor, my dark-haired, olive-skinned mother carried inner land mines of her own, which exploded periodically whenever I stepped near her wounded parts. Evacuated to Wales as a child, she suffered a perforated ulcer at eighteen, and lived anxiously unaware, even to herself, when the next blasted ulcer of the mind would explode inside and make itself known to the outside. On weekends, I'd take the bus and then the subway to the apartment she rented. Sometimes I'd have to knock and knock and knock on her door. I'd hear her stumble in her nightie to unlatch the chain on the locked door, and watch her body fall back into an overstuffed chair. She said, "I never should have left your father." I scurried about, recycling empty wine bottles, washing dishes, and emptying ashtrays, forcing outward order to bring calm to the small space.

When I was twelve, my mother told me that she'd kill me if I ever took up smoking. This advice scratched against my throat while I breathed in her second-hand smoke and the threat. I think she held the habit to avoid gaining weight while fears of cancer diagnoses came periodically into conversations about the most recent lump she had discovered or the neck pain she felt upon waking. She still believed her words would carry a different weight with me, and her body language didn't matter. She believed those threats to health and all the reasons why I should not smoke would somehow inoculate me against the impulse. I didn't want to smoke, but I inhaled the lesson and did anyway.

When I was six, I didn't have to plan or think about eating or running or deciding how to move my body through life. I'd burst through the front door after dinner, calling out as we climbed trees searching for friends playing hide and seek into the darkening night with the voice of my mother trailing behind, demanding me to be "more lady-like." The curves of the willow branches supported me while its tender boughs hid me from devouring eyes. Movement and motion flowed fearlessly with ease, without scripting. Breath merged with body untroubled, hunger grew naturally from abundance. The threats of war took up residence in

tissues not yet fully developed, not yet exercised in the language of post-war life. I don't remember getting explicit lessons for living in a body. Instead, I received covert messages about my body, about its utility for others, until later in life, when I noticed the ache in my left hip. My body had something to say.

When my body began to speak its own language, I had to listen. Language requires a speaker and a listener, a writer and a reader. I felt that mindless movement and compliance are like cancer cells growing restlessly. I could no longer ignore the increasing pain in my left hip with all its metaphors and symbolism. I researched the causes, read about

the mechanics of this pivotal joint, and realized that running played a role in revealing the pain whose source originated in another country, in another time. My physical body needed rest while the war within needed resolution. Some spiritual traditions speak of left hip pain as the signal of unresolved mother issues, or where the body feels stuck and cannot move forward. Running translated movements of my body. But running failed to teach me how to move with my body, how to translate the language of my parents residing in my body. Raised in the body language of two WW2 survivors, I needed to discover my own way to move.

When I was fifty, I realized that I'd always felt the tug of writing, that translating life's flow both physically and emotionally on the page had an allure, that writing brought some order to the mind. And, that order might contain past battles, some inner war yet unresolved, making its way from the inside to the outside. It might contain hidden histories and unacknowledged harm. Now, with only the slightest flowing movement, I take my pen and begin. Here, all of it can be included, all of it can find its place in story. Here, I find the stillness, moments of reflection where inheritance forms the foundation of a story, where conscious movement and deep emotional connections allow me to write with the language of my own body.

***

Bare with Me
by Rachel Brook

Saturday afternoon
on the sofa
I am unpicking stitches
to remove the sleeves from a shirt
(since it seems I prefer vests)

I feel I am forever
unpicking the stitches
stubbornly sewn by a world
that does not want me
to love or be as I am
but would prefer to entrap me
in one box or another

I poise the point of my unpicker
again and again and again
against an ornery overlocked seam
pulling with all my might
at tangled threads of misplaced expectation
that have webbed themselves around me

I have to believe
that with enough effort
every last stitch can be undone
and the unwanted sleeve cast off

I am an unpicker, a seam ripper
with every stitch I undo, I am
uncovering
discovering
fashioning

a fresh seam
richer and more welcoming
and far less stifling

Scarred Creatures
by Kristy Ettel

When I came to him, crying
after the masseuse came on me, smirking,
he asked why I had gone alone, said,
    "The hare that strays beyond her burrow
    courts the circling hawk."

When their whispers and whistles
struck my skirt like hurled stones, he laughed,
    "If the flower loathes the bees,
    why brandish such suggestive shades of yellow?"

When I sought refuge in his arms, he used them
to pin mine down.
    "Now now, a butterfly loses her beauty
    thrashing wings against metal bars."

Today, I kneeled to the earthworm, asked her
if I could join her under there,
safe from the sunlight, the air,
and the animals that call her prey—
that is to say, all of them. She replied,

"Even the dirt has its ways of scarring a creature,
but look how I tunnel, rescheming the ground, weaving
healing in quiet earth-darkness."

I run the hare past every fence,
teach the flower to close at dusk and heal,
sharpen the butterfly's wings against wire
until metal remembers it can bend.

Like the earthworm, through mire
I rise, released and wild,
to claim the open air as mine.

"Once your life is a conscious process, being blissful is natural, moving toward liberation is inevitable."
~ Sadhguru

Dragon's Eye
by Tim van Gardingen

How can I write the words to a tale defying all?
All truth or reason, all will to march its course,
And can I tether this responsibility to a source stronger than me?

How must I stare into the dragon's eye,
To catch a glimpse of my inner fire,
To meet such jealousy and turn it down with pride?

How did they live alone, those hermit saints of old?
Staring out from mountain peaks and seeking love inside
In their quest for presence, did they lose the ones beside?

And now I stand a saint with a road of coals to go.
Set to flame to lick the soles of my feet and my heart,
And please know this truly is my wish and choice.

How must I stare into the dragon's eye,
To catch a glimpse of my inner fire,
To meet such jealousy and turn it down with pride?

Deny their words, embrace your truth,
Lift your brow from mountain peaks,
Stand on coals, and dance.

I stared into the dragon's eye.
Will you follow me?

Silver and Gold

by Mars Gorman

Make new friends, but keep the old / one is silver and the other gold. / a circle is round, it has no end / that's how long I want to be your friend.

\- *Joseph Parry*

From a young age, we are taught that old friends are the most valuable, and that friendship is something that lasts forever. From songs like the one above to mass-produced matching "BFF" necklaces, these notions can be found everywhere in popular culture. Even as adults, our media is chock-full of dynamic duos who've known each other since kindergarten, whose deep and enduring love is based on a shared history.

But what about those of us who spent our formative years grappling with adverse circumstances, and our young adulthoods recovering from that trauma? We've all heard that, for a variety of complex psychological reasons, people who were abused growing up can follow similar patterns when choosing their romantic partners. However, I contend that this is true for all relationships, not just romantic ones. Old friends may not always be the people who are best for us, or who make us feel like our best selves. They may, instead, be people we stayed with because they were familiar and felt safe.

When I started my journey of reckoning with my trauma and learning how to care for myself without guilt, I began to see patterns in the people I formed close friendships with. They were people who dangled approval like a carrot on a stick in front of me, giving me the opportunity to "earn" it by acting to their standards. My undiagnosed OCD and my upbringing had given me an obsession with being "perfect" and "good." If I could have these qualities, then maybe I could avoid the crushing pain of disapproval, of making others upset. I was a classic people pleaser, and I primarily made friends with the people who responded to those desperate attempts to please.

For me, disagreements meant shouting and fighting rather than respectfully discussing a difference of opinion. So, naturally, I avoided truly authentic conversations. This behavior allowed me to fit in quite well with groups of people who seemed to be similarly obsessed with being "unproblematic." Rather than grapple with the inevitable reality that we are all imperfect humans who sometimes hurt others, make mistakes, and reinforce systems of oppression, these people used their social groups to create an image of themselves as "good people". Inclusion in the group meant that one was a good person; any significant transgressions would result in a person being cut out of the group entirely. In this way, these groups also provided me (and the others in them) with a sense of secure identity. It is far easier to outsource the work of deciding you're a good person to your friend group than to grapple with the choices that you're making every day.

At the same time, I was very conscious of the fact that my inclusion in this in-group of "good people" was conditional. I constantly felt like a slip-up could deem me to be "problematic," "toxic," or otherwise unlovable. And this wasn't just a product of my OCD brain — although that obviously contributed. I witnessed friends in our group get completely shunned by everyone else for a mistake, or sometimes even just whispers of problematic vibes. I also saw how difficult it was to try and maintain relationships with people once they carried these labels: not only were they excluded from social events, but hanging out with them was always accompanied by the fear that I was going to be labeled guilty by association, especially when they were competing for my attention and people-pleasing with my more "unproblematic" friends.

I saw these patterns repeat themselves in each of the friend groups I joined. And no matter how many "friends" like this I seemed to have, I constantly felt starved of real affection and connection. As Amanda Brown puts it in her incredible piece about the epidemic of constant communication,

> "Love should be something that strengthens you, not something that makes you feel like a shell of yourself, hollowed by the weight of someone else's expectations. Instead of allowing love to be a space of trust, it has, for many, become a performance – a constant proving, a fear of falling short."

That's what love was for me in these groups — something I earned by performing goodness and perfection as defined by my friends.

When I finally got treatment for my OCD and started my long journey towards healing, I began to grapple directly with the fact that I'm not, and can never be, perfect. And that the meat of life — the things that make it worth living — occurs in those spaces of discomfort where we accept the possibility that we could be wrong, mess up, hurt others, and be hurt ourselves. These moments of vulnerability and imperfection do not make us unlovable monsters — they make us human. And each of us, as humans, is inherently worthy of love.

The more I grappled with this, the more I found myself uncomfortable in my relationships with my friends. I felt like I couldn't be vulnerable and authentic with them because I couldn't be "wrong" with them, and certainly could never accuse them of being "wrong" unless I wanted our entire relationship to blow up. I noticed that even though my friends and I would posture towards vulnerability and authenticity, it was all a front. Substack writer for *Telling The Bees* alludes to this kind of posturing in their piece about_people turning to AI chatbots for companionship, mentioning that confiding in a virtual assistant rather than another human being is "perfect for those who perform vulnerability but refuse to engage in it." Turning to a chatbot that is literally programmed to validate and affirm you provides a similar safety to confiding only in friends who do the same.

One group of friends I lived with insisted on having monthly "roommate meetings" where we all checked in about our relationships and mental health. In reality, these meetings were exactly this kind of performance of vulnerability, where the stronger personalities at the table received validation from and doled out corrections to the people-pleasers. One such friend once threatened to cut another off during one of these meetings because the latter had spent "too long" being depressed about their grandmother's death.

The more energy I put into my therapy and my efforts to heal the wounds I'd been carrying since childhood, the more I was able to recognize that the motivations behind these corrections were less "tough love" and more attempts to coerce compliance with the social order we'd built. I recognized that I was participating in this cliquey behavior, too, using cruelty and judgement to try to influence others' behavior.

And it wasn't just negative feelings I felt I couldn't be vulnerable about with these friends. When I had joy or good news to share, their reactions were tepid at best. Other authors have written about how, in many social circles, taking joy and delight in things is seen as uncool or cringey. I could almost see my old friends comparing their situation to mine when I shared good news, calculating where my "win" placed me in relation to them. I noticed, too, that it felt like we never had any interesting discussions: we couldn't disagree with one another or bring up controversial topics.

I started to find that I didn't like the person that I was when I spent time with these people. But these were some of my oldest friends. The friendships that were supposed to last forever! My "gold" friends, friends I'd forged in the crucible of middle school, or future members of my bridal party I'd clicked with in my first year of college. Surely, the lessons I'd been taught in childhood couldn't have been wrong about how important these kinds of friendships were!

But the truth is, the friendships that satisfy our human need for connection and keep us from the deleterious effects of loneliness can be forged at any age, and aren't dependent on a bedrock of shared childhood or college finals week shenanigans. In an interview with Anya Meyerowitz for *Glamour*, therapist Emma Reed Turrell observes that it can actually be very healthy to transition from old relationships — which are often built on co-dependence due to the demands of adolescence — to new ones. There's even evidence to suggest that sticking with bad friendships can have detrimental outcomes for your mental health. Which makes perfect sense — of course, the quality of our relationships impacts our lives. But I think it's important to emphasize that quality is completely separate from quantity — that is, that relationships can be helpful or unhelpful to us regardless of how new or old they are.

The childhood lesson that we should stick it out in these "old" friendships is one that I had to confront directly and reject for my own mental health. There were so many societal pressures telling me I had to stand by my friends: from the feeling that I couldn't survive without the "gold" of old friendships, to the idea that I was supposed to be "ride or die" for them, to the assertion that the good qualities that I once saw in these people were still there deep down.

As Meyerowitz also explores, there's an undercurrent of pressure in our society based around the idea that if you *don't* have old friends, there must be something wrong with you. To put it the way my brain ruminated over and over again, quoting Tumblr user *gothicprep*,

> "before blaming others, think: whats the 1 constant in all your failed relationships? its that cursed egyptian amulet why do u even have that".

This obviously humorous subversion of an injunction to consider oneself as the common denominator in a series of failed relationships haunted me, whispering in my ear that there must be something fundamentally wrong with me if I kept making friends with people who turned out to be cruel towards me and others. But the truth is that there *was* something wrong with me — my "cursed amulet" were patterns I learned from traumatic experiences that led me to seek out friends who hurt me. Like victims of abuse who keep coupling with abusive partners, this pattern didn't mean it was my fault that these people had treated me poorly, it didn't mean that I had "failed" at being a friend, and it didn't mean there was something fundamentally wrong with me that made me undeserving of real friendship.

And the truth is that, even if you're going through life making only meaningful and healthy friendships, people come and go. That is the nature of life. It could be a move, a misunderstanding, a death, or any number of things out of our control that end a friendship. Sorry to the Spice Girls, but sometimes, friendship does end.

I've found a lot of comfort looking at the end of these old friendships in the same way my therapist and I talk about old, unhealthy coping mechanisms: as something that was helpful and perhaps even vital to my survival at one point in my life, but that I've since outgrown. I can and should cherish the good times that I had with my old friends. The fact that a friendship ended does not mean that it was a mistake in the first place: impermanence does not mean insignificance. I will always remember my middle school friends and I talking late into the night on swing sets, encouraging one another to follow our dreams, and making each other laugh uncontrollably about nothing. The memories I shared with them will always be gold, but by our mid-twenties, the reality of our relationship absolutely wasn't.

I wish I could say that I had all of these realizations, made the decision to leave my old friends, and vulnerably, but amicably, communicated these things to them, ending our friendships cleanly and beautifully while expressing gratitude for all we'd meant to one another. But the truth was, these were mostly realizations I had after I'd been kicked out of my friend groups and socially shunned in the way I'd seen other friends get shunned before me. These moments were emotionally devastating, but I was able to use them to reflect on what had gone wrong in these relationships and decide to break my cycle of attaching myself to people who demanded

compliance in exchange for approval. What has come out of that decision has been an incredibly fulfilling wealth of new friendships.

Sometimes, silver is better than gold. Sometimes, losing all your old friends — which can feel like the end of the world — is actually the beginning of your journey into more fulfilling relationships. Novelty is extremely beneficial to the human brain; meeting new people, expanding your horizons, and encountering new ideas gives your mind a hit of dopamine. Even if we don't agree with someone, our brains are stretched when we try to understand where they're coming from rather than shutting them out immediately for being different from us.

This is how we grow, how we become more than what we were taught to be in childhood. Not to mention that building strong community ties_with people who are different from us is one of the achievable ways we can resist our current fascist government. Community is built when people come together and share ideas. Community is built when you talk to your neighbors, work through your disagreements, and show vulnerability.

I'll be the first to admit that trying to make new friends can also be extremely scary. Because I'm a nerd, I've been reading a lot about it to try to make it easier for myself. Abrams and Brown argue that the hard truth is that to make new friends, we do have to stretch ourselves to have awkward conversations with strangers. The good news about these conversations is that studies suggest that people actually enjoy them more than they think they will, and initiating them can become easier with as little as a week of consistent practice.

My new friends have so much to teach me in ways that I wouldn't have otherwise considered. Like my new friend from the community garden who taught me how to identify rat burrows (thanks, Andrew!) or my friend from work who gave me the idea of carrying a lavender sachet around in my purse (thanks, Jarrod!). Perhaps most importantly, meeting and interacting with new friends helps to remind me that I am not on this earth to be quiet and perfect and never make mistakes. I am here to experience new things, mess up, learn how to love, and be a flawed human being in a big and beautiful world full of other flawed human beings.

***

Exceptional Man

by Emmanuel Ezendu

Handsome men wonder from where my strength lies
I'm not cute or heavily built to win a prize
But when I start to brief them, all I hear are cries
I say,
It is in the cushion of my mind;
The calm in my voice,
The confidence in my steps behind,
The solitude in my noise.
I'm a man
Exceptionally;
Exceptional man,
That's me.

I step into a place
Composed even to my foes
And to a woman's face.
They rise like fans or fall down on their toes
I say,
It is in the furnace in my eye pupils,
The flesh in my muscles
The depth in my dimples
The joy in my hustles
I'm a man
Exceptionally;
Exceptional man, that's me.

Women sit, yet can't breach
What they see in me
They struggle to reach
But they still can't see
My inner mystery
When I try to point it
All I say is history.
I say,
It is in the romance in my tone
The hope in my smile
The love in my zone
The wisdom in my style
I'm a man
Exceptionally.
Exceptional man,
That's me.

Now you see
Why my head is not hung in shame.
Take it or let it be;
It is not about riches or fame,
But about who I am.
So, when next you see me,
I ought to brighten your star.
I say,
It is the curl of my hair
The beauty in my color
The power in my stare
The fearlessness in my valor
'Cause I'm a man
Exceptionally;
Exceptional man
That's me!

Inspired by Maya Angelou, one of my favorite poets.

transformation

noun / træns.fəˈmeɪ.ʃən /

a complete change in the appearance or character of something or someone, especially so that that thing or person is improved.

Old Family Magic

by Mary M. Brown

He taught you
to disappear
when you
were with him,
schooled you

in the safety
of silence
since your voice
set him off,
sent him

back to some
earlier time,
to Vietnam
or an even earlier
war,

the service he
had enlisted in
long before
you became his
bomb

Now that he
is gone, you
are in shock
at how real
your grief

is, how
explosive
your pain You
discover it on
your face

in the mirror
when you
finally see
yourself
reappear

Mediumsinart:
A Space that Defines Violence. Reclaiming Voice. Speaking the Unspoken.

Mediumsinart's primary mission is to give essential structure and accurate definitions to sexual violence. They are attempting to negate prejudiced cultural and religious attitudes and arbitrary social criteria
for defining instances of sexual, physical and emotional violence against girls and women.

Kathleen Hoy Foley, a victim of sexual violence herself, expands and deepens the voice of the female experience.
Raw. Uncompromising. Compassionate. Deliberately antagonistic. Kathleen writes to awaken the courage within the reader.

Kathleen delivers a trilogy traversing the landscape of traumatic abuse, each demonstrating truth as the path to freedom:
Woman in Hiding, which speaks of truth as personal and social advocacy.
Breaking Through Silence discusses the truth as mentorship and education.
And *Forget About Heaven*, told through a series of individual monologues uniting the physical and spiritual planes. The book addresses our souls' enduring dedication and indestructible devotion to their inherent calling of love.

Her books are offered free to anyone.
To download a PDF copy of Kathleen's books, and read her blog or her Poetic Imagery, visit her website:

www.mediumsinart.weebly.com

Image below:
How Do You Die?
by Rachel Lorraine

Poem.

How do you die,
A little at a time or all at
once?
How many times and
how often?
What is necessary in
Becoming..

It's dalia season.. The
scent transcends
melancholic phrase and
haze of why we're here..
Accomplishment? How
thin. How purposeless
in the guise of true
imprint.
What are we truly left
with? Do we still not
know?

We still look for leads to
follow, foreign to our
own compass, allowing it
to rust in our
conditioned distrust.
The distance between
where we exist and
where we must go-
covered with material
debris to reroute
destination, mislead our
trajectory to reflect a
victory.. against
ourselves.

...cont'd. from page 35

K: We are more powerful than we are told to believe. Has your art changed alongside you as you've grown, healed, or evolved personally?

R: My art and expressions have evolved alongside me. It took me a long while to own the title of Artist, which is funny as it's all I've ever been. For a while, I was just labeled a painter, even that was hard to own for a time. I always did art, I always wrote poetry, but to claim it as an identity - I didn't feel I was worthy (programming). That shifted as I worked to shed imposed perfectionism and imposter syndrome and cultivate Self worth. I still wrestle with its echo, but it doesn't warp me any longer. And as I discovered the healing nature of photography and self-portraiture, I moved rapidly through that development, as I viewed it as an opportunity to go deeper, faster - bringing another depth of the internal to the external. Again, peeling back the armor that hid me until all that was left was Me. Just me. My thoughts. My words. My imagery. My truth. Each expression removes a bar from my cage. Now I can see the sky, and I watch the trees dance above me and the birds sing...I've created a view I was meant to see - and I will keep dismantling, until I can See it all.

K: Speaking of dismantling, what was one small act of resistance in your life that turned out to be profoundly powerful?

R: The moment I took action, ownership and a stand for Self in an intentional and defined way, was indeed a turning point for me in my early 20s. It Shifted the trajectory of my self-worth, my internal/external freedom and set the foundation for my long journey of Self creation and embodiment; the first step in acknowledging, allowing and loving Myself. It was profound for me and the memory surreal, like a dream or film. My wisest, greatest act of Self love was in resistance and release of an imposed identity and a welcoming home to Myself. In the moment of my reclamation, I was asked in confusion by the powers that be in this setting, "Wouldn't this open a lot of doors for you?" My response - "No doors that I wish to enter, sir." And I walked out in full alignment with my head held higher than it had ever been. In this movie moment, I emerged for air for the first time from a life lived underwater, and finally found land, severing the anchor at my feet. I am still so proud of that brave girl and grateful for her foresight and courage.

K: That is amazing! I am still practising saying no to all the things that don't align with me. One thing I have found challenging, while also life-changing, is to be able to distinguish between my ego voice and my soul voice. One is fed from external validation, while the other, the soul's intuition, feeds off a deeper knowing that what is best for me is not found in a box. Is there a part of yourself you're learning to embrace more fully these days?

R: I'm always learning and in active practice to embrace and embody myself more fully so I can alchemize inherited shame and evaporate narratives that poison the well - for we drink from this well and claim nourishment, then wonder why we are angry, hateful and sick all the time...in a world drowning in unkindness and disconnection. To cleanse it, it starts with how we hydrate Self. It takes much work to unlearn, rewrite and Live the existence of soul's design, as one is meant to live by, but worth every second of its challenges. I'm lovingly learning to embrace my quirks and the storyline of often being misunderstood, causing the creation of false narratives. It takes much bravery and continuous kindness and patience to honor oneself fully - the parts that cause trouble in your life, things you were bullied for, things I learned to assign shame to or wished didn't exist in me and opposing labels that are born from another's personal Need to see me through Their cracked lens...But the thing is, we are no different from one another, and all hold onto these self-narratives imposed by mind or matter. We all fall into our toxic training of unjust judgements and projections-fears. There is not a soul that does not stand without misunderstanding, labeling or projection. And I am always working towards making peace with that reality and not letting its existence dismantle my trajectory. To coexist freely with this shadow. To allow oneself to be Seen is to be interpreted by another's conditioned perception-most won't get it right. Release the need for control. Embrace being misunderstood. Not everyone will See you in this life, and I'm learning that's ok. I am safe, regardless.

K: Going back to your art, what themes or ideas are you most interested in exploring through your work?

R: There's this quote I kept on my mirror in my studio, always stuck with me - "All human beings should try to learn before they die what they are running from, and to, and why," by James Thurber. I believe in this deeply. I have always been intrigued with what people fear, how and why, as it shapes who we are, how we treat others and who we define ourselves to be - consciously or subconsciously...what is deemed as "ugly" or "dark", "slutty" or "wrong" or just merely inspires discomfort and gossip...but why? Who told us such things - how were they born and why do YOU believe them? Is it truly your judgement to carry? We are all traumatized by tales we allow as identity. Everything stems from something - early conditioning, generational traumas, pain, grief... inspiring collected narratives; Societal, universal, historical, inherited and self-erected stories and tall tales we rule our modern lives by. I find it imperative to explore the depths of these grounds, dig up the earth and get dirty in doing it. If we neglect our whole Selves, part vacant and foreign to ALL we are, due to fear and what was taught, are we not merely a shell of this existence? Half known, half realized and limited by choice. Isn't this the point: To know, embody and embrace all we are in this life? So, to be fully Alive while living? And in

Image below:
Voices Of Woman.
by Rachel Lorraine

Self portrait.

doing so, we can then allow ourselves to hold the same space, honor and intention for others. This is the ground floor of my expressions; deep in the pit of excavation in search of wholeness, fullness, and to show, though afraid, it should not stop one from exploring who they Are; to adapt to our findings and learn we can allow love for what's buried beneath the rubble. In doing so, I believe it will shape a much kinder world. To fear oneself is a most tragic and damaging thing, and sadly, most common - as its roots exposed to light by how we treat each other...because it's how we treat ourselves.

K: Exactly! And perfectly stated. Are there particular causes, values, or messages that you feel compelled to highlight through your art?

R: I touch upon many topics and themes in my work. Pairing self-portrait photography or oil paintings with my poetry, as I feel several avenues of expression united, roots and embodies the message of a piece I'm moved to challenge and convey. I like to look at the elephant in the room square on, as it often feels I'm the only one who sees it, and peer behind the veil to see the soul of a matter. I do that through the lens of my emotions. I touch upon issues most like not to think of, and turn them into beautiful awareness and reflection, if I may be that conduit. Themes such as: realities of the human condition - "unwanted" emotions, injustice, abuse, trauma, shame, organized religion, misogyny, societal oppressions, labels/pressures placed upon Women, discrimination, survival...etc. Ironically, they all hold threads from the same cloth. But I also expose light on beautiful things; Hope, Women's Rights, body empowerment, Nature, Humanity & Equality, strength, courage, t he ability to heal oneself. Self love and universal love. Awareness. Safety in acceptance. Bravery to evolve, expansion. Growth. Revolution. Unity. Connection. Mother Earth...Again - same cloth.

K: Looking ahead, what stories are calling to you now? What's next on your creative horizon?

R: I don't confine myself to logical time, which can be strange in this society...but time is Now. Moment by moment, in the present we exist, so it is difficult for me to step into future foresight and plan deep ahead. I get ideas I can't activate yet and store within me until I create space to birth them. I have desires to show more work in galleries and do poetry readings, connect more personally and openly with community. Work with more clients to know and imprint their beautiful stories. Uncover more bravery and honesty as I step forward, continuing to unlock doors previously bolted shut, for myself and for others. There is much to explore...and I am grateful and excited for all that awaits me.

***

You can learn more about Rachel below:

Instagram: @visual.maiden

Image above:
When My Myth Has Failed...
by Rachel Lorraine

Self portrait.

Learning to Breathe

by Margaret Gibbs

I often think about how long I've spent hating my body. How many years spent tugging at skin, white imprints left in pink flesh, wishing I could push around bone and fat and skin for the perfect body. Now, I miss the teenage body I once concealed under oversized clothes and behind crossed arms — the irony is delicious. Is this what the rest of my life is to be: wishing for a body that no longer exists and cannot ever again?

I can't name the moment when I suddenly became aware of my protruding belly, the one my mom would tickle and call my "Madame Alexander" belly after the dolls. But one day, I started sucking it in and never stopped. My mom once told me this is why women never get that "beer belly" old men have, because we've been engaging our cores since we were children. She didn't see the irony in what she was saying. But I heard and felt it. Even now, I feel it, when I breathe, I am trained to breathe up instead of out.

When I try to make myself breathe in and out, letting my belly expand, filling my lungs to capacity, it feels wrong. Tight. Like pleura won't slide. Breath hitches, trapped between inhalation and exhalation. But stomach taut, always pulled in.

In these moments, I'm transported back to the pool where my Nana taught swimming for thirty years. She taught thousands of kids to swim, including my siblings and me. To keep us from inhaling or drinking the water, we learned to blow bubbles.

Blow, blow, blow.

Kick, kick, kick.

Then came holding your breath.

I don't remember learning how to swim, but I have pictures of it. Me, at two years old at Hilton Head Island, a swim bubble attached to my back as I lay on my stomach in the shoreline, eyes shut, smiling with my crooked, pacifier teeth. Back when my smile traveled all the way to my eyes, not just my mouth. Pictures of my mom in a bikini - and smiling all the way to her eyes. My nana, in the midst of her Weight Watcher's obsession. All of us on the beach, building sandcastles with a version of my dad I've never seen, or at don't least remember. But again and again, I notice the weight and the weightlessness of my siblings and me. The easy fullness of our bodies. Our stomachs poking out below tankinis, arms soft with baby fat, remnants of a time when we were nourished without question or condition. I see the innocence and freedom of our bodies, free from the pressing, the pulling, the tucking.

We did not yet know to critique ourselves in the mirror, did not yet know to fear the way our thighs spread when we sat in the sand or the way our bellies rounded when we laughed too hard. We ran with abandon, flung ourselves into waves, collapsed onto towels with bad tan lines and salt-dried hair, never questioning if we had the right to take up space. Our bodies were full of joy, of movement, of discovery. We did not press or pull or suck in or wish them into something else.

But the years changed that. Slowly, imperceptibly, the innocence of our bodies slipped away. I can track our journeys with our bodies through our annual beach pictures. The way our bodies shift and stretch, how they carry time like

> "It is about self-worth, about legacy, about the quiet ways we are taught to shrink."

footprints in the sand, washed over and redrawn, but never quite the same. In those fleeting moments captured on film, I notice, most of all, the growing discomfort in our bodies. The way my sister shifts and then contorts her body to appear as small as possible. The arm that slowly comes up to guard my brother's chest until the next year, there is a swim shirt in its place. Arms start to cross over stomachs, hands rest strategically at waists, and towels wrap around shoulders before the camera clicks. We learned, somewhere along the way, that bodies are to be managed, sculpted, hidden. That softness is to be hardened, and confidence is conditional.

And yet, the ocean does not care. The waves do not shrink from the fullness of our forms, the tide does not turn away from our insecurities. The beach has seen us through all our transformations, the childlike freedom, the awkward self-consciousness, the hesitant reclamation of self. No matter how we have changed, the ocean has welcomed us all the same, cradled us in its endless rhythm.

I wonder what it would be like to reclaim the body I once had, not in form, but in spirit alone. To live inside myself without constant evaluation, without chronic dissatisfaction. To believe, once again, that my body exists not to be gazed upon or judged, but simply to carry me through this life. I want to feel that easy fullness again, that natural weight of existence, unburdened by shame. But I am not a child anymore, and the world has shaped me differently. The voices, the images, the expectations, they sit heavy on my skin and live in my bones.

This tension did not begin with me. My grandmother has cycled through diets her entire life, a pendulum swinging between extremes. She had a binge eating disorder, losing and regaining the same weight over and over again, never satisfied, always chasing an impossible ideal. My grandmother's weight was always a topic of conversation, spoken about in hushed tones, in concern-tinged judgment. I can still hear my mother's voice describing her mother's eating habits with a mix of pity and disdain. How many times have I heard the same tone used to describe my own choices? My dad, once a long-distance runner with a body built for endurance, struggles now with a weight that will not budge. My mom, the kind of woman who can live on an almond a day, whose discipline around food is both enviable and terrifying, passed down her restriction. My sister and I inherited not just her features, but also her anxieties. Both of us have battled disordered eating in different forms, internalizing the lessons spoken and unspoken: that thinness is virtuous; that control is everything.

It is not just about food. It is about self-worth, about legacy, about the quiet ways we are taught to shrink. My mom, the woman who taught me to suck in my stomach and breathe up instead of out, still looks at herself with a critical eye, still lives in fear of indulgence. We are all caught in this cycle, all part of the same quiet shrinking passed down through generations.

Still, I try. I try to step into the ocean like I once did, letting the water rise around me, letting it remind me that I am not as rigid as I think. That I am fluid, shifting, capable of change. I try to breathe without restriction, to let my stomach rise and fall as it was meant to, without the constant pull of self-consciousness. I try to look at old pictures not with regret or longing, but with gratitude for the body that carried me then and the body that carries me now.

I do not want to spend my life mourning versions of myself I failed to love. I do not want to look back, ten years from now, and wish I had loved this body while I had it. So, I remind myself, again and again, that I am more than my reflection. That the size of my waist, the softness of my arms, and the roundness of my belly, these are not measures of my worth. That my body is not an ornament but a vessel. And vessels are meant to be filled with breath, with laughter, with the simple pleasures of life.

So, I try. I stand at the edge of the water, feet sinking into the wet sand, and I let the tide come in. And for a moment, just a moment, I feel weightless again.

***

Quickening
by Regina Berg

This world is full of wolves who swallow
little girls whole, then cough up the living bones
of women their stomachs could not hold.

The world is full of the clatter of those bones
gathering earth to flesh themselves, standing
among wolves unafraid, knowing that these bones

can survive hell, can survive the bellies of wolves, and
that once eaten, we can never be afraid
in that way again. Our bones re-membering.

Our nimble fingers quickening ourselves. Building
feet arched and fleet, building calves and thighs,
bellies and breasts, arms and shoulders

thick and supple as the roots of trees, building
the backs of others in places that they cannot
reach, cannot see the missing muscle or skin

and all of this in the presence of wolves.
For we have found in our re-fleshing, stones and
rocks and great boulders that our hands

have crafted into instruments that are delicate and beautiful
and lethal. If wolves are not afraid of the power of our bodies, let them
understand the power of death.

In Doc Martens, Not High Heels

by Taslym Umar

I've never written a personal essay before. This will be my first—if I ever gather enough courage to actually send it in. Why the hesitation? Well, personal essays are a form of self-expression, and in my community, that's basically the equivalent of streaking in the town square. Especially if you're a woman. Or a girl. Or anyone with ovaries, really.

To be fair, the society I grew up in isn't your stereotypical ultra-strict Muslim community where girls get stoned for breathing near a man. This isn't Saudi or Iran, where talking to a guy gets you side-eyed into oblivion. No, my society encourages you to talk to men. Because how else are you supposed to land a husband before you expire at 25?

Marriage is the endgame. Like Thanos. Only with more lace and less mercy.

Here, the aunties won't stone you. They'll do worse. They'll talk. About your weight (or your lack thereof), your skin tone, your laugh, your shoes—basically your entire existence. The gossip moves faster than the flies buzzing around our overcrowded compounds. And if looks could kill? Babe, we'd all be statistics.

Perfection is demanded — but only from women, obviously. The men get participation trophies for existing.

This is a society built by men, for men. A place where a woman's mistake—be it a slip of the tongue or a slip of hijab—becomes a full-blown scandal.

Now picture me: an awkward, anxious, slightly-too-loud girl who trips over her abaya and her words. A raging Swiftie with social anxiety. A girl who once asked a Malam in Islamiyya if jinns pay rent, expecting the class to burst out laughing. Spoiler: the class didn't laugh. The Malam didn't smile. I got flogged—not the gentle kind, either. The "this child is definitely possessed" kind. I cried all the way home. And I didn't dare tell my mum. I was scared I'd get a second round of beatings just for embarrassing the family with my "weird" questions.

I was a quiet kid — not the angelic, bookish kind, but the terrified-of-getting-shouted-at kind. You know, the kind who says "sorry" when an adult steps on her foot. My default mode was obedient. "Yes, Auntie." "Okay, Mama." "Of course, Malam." I said yes so much I almost forgot the word no existed.

Politeness was currency. Disobedience? That was social bankruptcy.

The women around me were emotional gymnasts—balancing everyone's needs, expectations, and unsolicited opinions while forgetting they had names outside of "Mummy," "Aunty," or "Wife." They passed this down like an heirloom:

"Don't talk back."

"Don't question."

"Smile politely."

"Say thank you when they insult you."

(Okay, maybe not that last one—but you get the vibe.)

It wasn't just about being "a good girl." It was survival. Your worth was measured by how little you complained. How much you endured. How invisible you could make your anger.

But I was tired of swallowing my voice like cough syrup.

There were signs I was glitching in the programming. I remember being 14, watching a Kannywood movie where the girl ran away to chase her dreams — and I clapped. I didn't even realize I was clapping until my mum gave me a look like I'd barked during Qur'an recitation. That was my villain origin story, I think.

But maybe the glitches started earlier. I remember being a little girl, riding in my father's car —much to my mother's dismay—and screaming my lungs out for no reason. Picture it: a six-year-old in pigtails, face squished against the window, screeching her ears out like a tiny banshee. Looking back, I think I was just screaming out all that bottled-up chaos and unspoken trauma. Naturally, that earned me the title of "crazy girl"—a reputation that, weirdly enough, kept me somewhat unscathed. The overly judgmental aunties didn't even bat an eyelash at the things I did. They just nodded and said, "Ah, yes, that makes sense for her." Of course, my mum didn't find it as charming. That reputation earned me more beatings than I can count.

Around that time, I started listening to Taylor Swift under my hijab. Yes, Taylor. Blondie had me in a chokehold. Her lyrics were like therapy in 3 minutes and 45 seconds. "Shake It Off" was my anthem—because I had a lot to shake off, okay?

Every act of resistance was small, but it was mine. Not wearing makeup to school despite the girls' judgmental looks. Asking questions that made my teachers sweat. Being best friends with a boy. Laughing too loudly in public. Wearing Doc Martens with my abaya because I refused to trip gracefully.

I know what you're thinking: "That's not even rebellious." But if you grew up in a society like mine, those were full-blown revolutions.

So yeah, I didn't grow up burning bras or staging protests (no bras to burn anyway). But I broke rules. Quietly. Softly. Like a girl whispering no for the first time—and realizing the world didn't end. It just... shifted.

Then came the ultimate test: marriage.

"...have crafted into instruments that are delicate and beautiful and lethal. If wolves are not afraid of the power of our bodies, let them understand the power of death."
~ Regina Berg

I was barely out of university when the family started rolling out their husband shortlists like resumes. The aunties brought forth The One. You know the One—tall, respectable, religious (on paper), and absolutely not my vibe. I was supposed to pray istikhara and convince myself that his voice sounding like a goat with asthma was just part of Allah's test.

But my heart wasn't in it.

Then came Isah. A quiet civil engineer who didn't flinch when I told him Taylor Swift was my favorite artist. I braced myself for a Hadith quote or a judgmental stare. But he just shrugged and said, "She's actually pretty poetic."

That was it. That was my istikhara. The green light I didn't know I was waiting for.

So, imagine me: the quiet girl, the die-hard people pleaser, choosing not to marry the guy my mother and aunties approved of, and standing my ground. I said no to tradition. I said yes to someone who saw me. Not just the wife-shaped silhouette they wanted me to be.

The family drama that followed? Whew. Let's just say if looks could kill, I'd have been buried in lace.

But I held my ground. And for the first time in my life, it didn't feel like rebellion. It felt like healing.

Because breaking the cycle isn't always loud. Sometimes it's a whisper. Sometimes it's choosing love over obligation. Doc Martens over heels. Self-respect over politeness.

I still have social anxiety. I still flinch when older women give me the up-down scan of disapproval. But I laugh loudly now—and mean it. I wear my Swiftie badge with pride. I married the man who respects my weird questions and doesn't treat me like a malfunctioning robot when I cry for no reason.

I broke the cycle. Not in flames. But in fragments. In tiny, deliberate acts of rebellion that pieced together the version of me that I actually want to be.

The good girl is gone.

And in her place is a woman who shakes it off, unapologetically.

***

Fraudulent Offerings

by Solomonn Ok

Do not give me fraudulent libations
After I poured myself and soul
At your feet and on your altars.
Maybe I was stupid for
    Making you my god.
Writing my poems as hymns
And my stories as myths.

I was malnourished because
I stopped eating from your hand.
What you offered made my stomach hurt.

I was meant to be worshipped, too.
Be dressed in golden bangles
    And bracelets.
To be vested in silk.
To wear hoops as big as moons.

Do the juices still run down your chin
From the fruits I offered?
Do the candles on your altar still burn?

Why should I keep your name in my prayers,
When you left my altars bare?

The Power (and Necessity) of Healing Out Loud

by Tinamarie Cox

I often find comfort in hearing my voice through someone else's words. Knowing you are not alone in a situation is a vital addition to the healing process. Too many times, I've gaslighted myself, thought I had to be crazy, or felt certain that no one else understood me. It's a consequence of people-pleasing. By denying myself, I sacrificed my well-being.

When you've been conditioned from childhood to put others before yourself, you learn to stuff your personal feelings deep down to keep the peace. You convince yourself that your needs just aren't as important, and you end up broken down on the side of the road. Eventually, you will run out of gas (motivation/ spark/ desire/ spirit/ vitality/ vivacity) and find yourself stuck somewhere between who you wish you were and who everyone expects you to be. You can't judge the distance correctly, but you know that one state of being feels closer, easier to reach, than the other. However, you only have enough energy to walk toward one.

You either choose to settle in Others' Expectations, a place you are more familiar with, or move along to Authentic Living. Despite the discomfort of moving to a new place in life, it's still tempting. And believe it or not, it's okay to ask for directions and opinions. You don't have to listen to everyone's advice, but it's always wise to welcome words from someone who's also travelled a similar path in life.

I continue to keep to myself, mostly (another behavior I was conditioned into, and I am trying to break). But my roots and curiosity have always run deep, deeper than I dared to show through my branches above ground during my younger years. A lot of my growth has taken place silently (underground and in my thought patterns), through the words of others, through reading.

I follow professional Instagram accounts, find therapeutic memes on Facebook, and read a Self-Help or Psychology-based book from the library regularly. I have this nagging desire to know "why is that?" I constantly seek more knowledge while on the quest to understand myself and the world around me (especially, people I can't directly relate to). These methods of acquisition I can do privately, at my own pace, and level of comfort and comprehension. And I am finally capable of letting my personal growth show through my freshly bloomed flowers.

I'd say I'm close to summer now.

I am budding and blooming every day, but I haven't reached my peak in beauty just yet. I'm on the cusp of living my best life because I chose to walk to the next town and explore Authentic Living. Reading, for me, was the equivalent of asking for directions. Therapy helped, too. And there was some medication in there to help fill the tank as well.

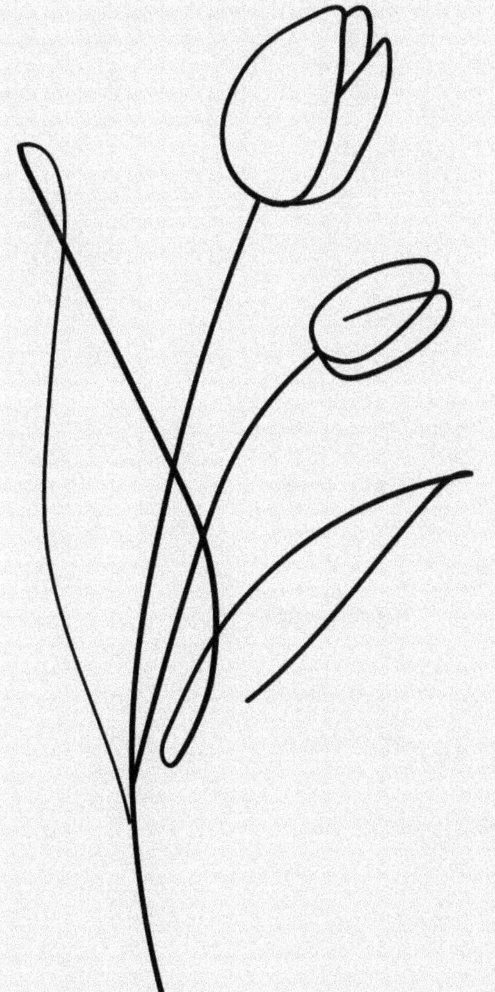

But every piece of work I've soothed my wounded self with was a tight hug I didn't realize I needed, until I felt paired with someone else's experience. It was hard to accept the embrace at times, again, because I desperately wanted to hold on to the fantasy of Others' Expectations being the safer home to live in. It was a place that didn't require me to show my face, something that could have made me feel embarrassed, ashamed, or rejected. And I went about my day under the Everyman mask, denying my individuality and self-sovereignty.

Others' Expectations was a place where I blended into the background neatly, invisibly, and quietly. I was easier to swallow because I could become anyone's cup of tea. And I thought being palatable meant I could (would) be genuinely loved. But one day, my skin started to crawl, and I knew I had developed an allergy to the masks. Through the words of others, I learned that I wasn't the only one with this allergy. I wasn't the only one who wanted to move out of the town I grew up in.

I have my own words now, thanks to the ones who healed out loud. I have a voice that complements my face. A song that matches how I dance. I live in a place where divergence is something to celebrate and encourage. A lot of people aren't ready to live here. And that's okay, so long as no one tries to take me back to where I started from.

***

Gain Hold Again

by V. Bray

I am now free to explore
    curves I never noticed
    fantasies I never thought to

Dream

in touch   my hands are new

memories pushed away

without my inner linings   that desire

for a certain kind of ecstasy
                disappears

I am no vessel   no fertile object
                to be used

my fingers slip   gain hold again

I create myself   anew

Body; The Mirror

by Rachel Turney

Body

I remember the body of my grandmother. In her floral dresses, sitting in a pew. I also remember her body naked, completely bare, in her later years. I don't wear floral dresses and I don't sit in pews. But, my body is the same as hers. I can see the similarities in every curve.

The Mirror

The mirror holds no mystery. I see exactly the same thing each day. The predictability of the passing of time, written there for all to see. I used to dance before the mirror in my small outfits before sailing off into the night. Now I pass the mirror quickly because I am busy. I don't stand for hours admiring myself as I once did. I don't sit before the mirror and labor with hot rods and eye liner. I don't peer at my own eyes. It's not because I am not pretty anymore, but it is because I am not lonely anymore. I do not need to connect with that girl in the mirror because she is with me all the time, and now I spend my minutes on other things. I brush my hair quickly, I apply mascara while pulling on my shoes. I look at the mirror only long enough to say hello to myself and then I move on. I don't meet with her in the darkness. I don't talk to her. I don't spend hours alone staring at myself in the mirror, anymore.

Safety
by Hailey Fiske

"Julie!" Josh yelled from the kitchen. "Where's the milk? Are we out already?" Julie gave herself one last glance in the mirror, choosing to ignore how unkempt her hair looked. She hurriedly grabbed her tote bag and swung it around her shoulder. Keys, keys, keys, Julie thought, slowly inspecting her room. There. She leaned down and snatched them from the spot where they lay on her carpet by the bed. She rushed out of her room, quickly making her way to the front door.

"Julie?" She stopped and glanced behind her. "The milk?" Josh said, waving his empty cereal bowl in her face. Julie fought the urge to roll her eyes.

"Did you look in the fridge, Josh?" She said, "I'm late, I have to go." She reached for the door again, but felt Josh's hand grab her shoulder, his grip tight. He pulled her back, forcing her to turn around and face him.

"Did I look in the fridge? What do you think? Do you think I'm some sort of idiot?" Josh said, his tone rising with anger. Julie winced and took a deep breath.

"Sorry, no. I think we're out, I'll pick some up on my way home." Julie muttered.

"Damn it, what am I supposed to eat? There isn't a crumb of food left in this godforsaken place." Josh said, finally letting go of her.

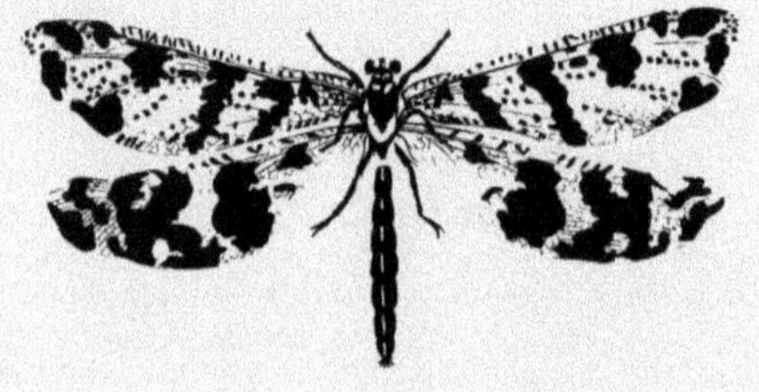

"I think we have some granola bars in the cupboard," Julie said, once again turning to leave.

"Get me a twelve-pack while you're at it," Josh said, walking back towards the kitchen. Julie rushed out of the door and hurried down the driveway. She glanced at her watch, but the digital face didn't light up. She fiddled with it for a moment, not stopping her stride.

*

"Damn," Julie muttered to herself. The watch had been on the fritz since she got it. She found it on some knock-off discount website. Julie resorted to rummaging around in her tote bag to grab her cell phone to check how late she was going to be to the shop. She felt around the random junk that was sitting in the bottom of her bag, but she didn't feel her phone. Crap. No phone, no knowing how late she truly was. She half-jogged down the street, trying to get to the subway as fast as she could. It was a few blocks, but she thought she might be able to make it. If she was late again, there was no way of knowing what her boss would do.

Julie finally reached the entrance to the subway and hurried down the stairs, weaving in between strangers who were taking their own sweet time. She rushed around the corner while simultaneously grabbing her credit card from her bag. She was lucky enough to find the wallet on the first attempt. She pulled her credit card out and paid the fee. Julie walked to her usual stop and stopped dead in her tracks. Oh no. She watched in horror as the subway car sped away, without her on it. She slumped her shoulders in defeat and found a bench to sit on. The next car should be there in about five minutes, but those were precious minutes that Julie couldn't lose. She had already been late three times this week.

She waited on the bench while anxiety flitted around in her stomach. The next train pulled to a stop. Julie made her way on the train, not bothering to rush. Her body was smashed between a woman who looked like she was going to browse the fancy boutiques downtown, and a tall man who reeked of weed and texted on his phone. The subway was usually like this. A variety of strangers, all with different agendas for the day. She'd unfortunately encountered a lot worse in her time on this train. Eventually, they reached her stop. Julie walked to the shop, rushing again, so her boss knew that she was at least attempting to get there on time.

She swung the door open, the bell above her head chiming. She kept her head down, avoiding eye contact with two of her coworkers who were already displaying arrangements of flowers in the window. Julie didn't have time to appreciate the beauty of the flowers. She knew her coworkers would exchange judgy glances, both sharing the same apprehension towards Julie. She went to the back of the shop and hung her canvas tote in the break room. She pulled her green apron off the rack, and quickly tied it around her.

> "With Julie's life being the way it was, the only thing she could count on was spending her day around nature's splendor. They kept her safe temporarily, graciously giving her shelter."

"Julie."

She turned towards the door, where her boss stood with her arms crossed.

"You are late. Again," Sharon said, pointing to the clock on the wall behind Julie. She turned to see that it was already 7:30. Her shift started at 7:00.

"Sharon, I am so sorry. I missed the train somehow and couldn't find my keys. No milk..." Julie trailed off, wringing her hands in front of her.

"Come to my office, we have to talk." Sharon turned and walked away, expecting Julie to follow. Julie filled with dread, knowing that the topic of this conversation wasn't going to be a good one. She followed Sharon to her office across the hall and sat down across from her desk. "Julie, we can't keep playing this game. You're late, and there's always an excuse. I forgive you and give you the benefit of the doubt. Yet, you continue to show up late," Sharon said, leaning forward in her chair, her elbows resting on the desk.

"I know, I know. I-"

"Julie, I can't keep you here anymore."

Julie paused and looked away, feeling her throat start to tighten and her eyes burn. She can't say that she didn't expect this, but she needed this job. She brought her sleeve to her eyes as tears started making their way down her face.

"I'm sorry, but you're half an hour late today, and it's been twenty minutes almost every day since I hired you. We have things to get done in the morning, and I need my staff to be here on time. You'll get the rest of last week's pay sent to you," she said, sounding genuinely sorry. Julie understood, you can't keep employees who never show up on time. But she desperately needed this job. She sniffled and took a deep breath.

"Sharon, please. I need this job. I'm begging you. Please."

"There are plenty of other places that can hire you, but I can't keep you on the staff. You can go now."

Julie stood up slowly, untying her apron.

"I am an unpicker, a seam ripper
with every stitch I undo, I am
uncovering
discovering
fashioning"
~ Rachel Brook

"Here," Julie said, holding the apron out to Sharon. She took it and gave her a pity-filled smile, saying nothing more.

Julie left the office, heading back to the breakroom. She grabbed her bag and walked onto the sales floor. She paused to take in the beauty of the flowers one last time. The roses, all of them, displayed perfectly. The peonies, daisies, and baby's-breath. She would miss them. With Julie's life being the way it was, the only thing she could count on was spending her day around nature's splendor. They kept her safe temporarily, graciously giving her shelter. Now, that sense of safety was gone. She walked through the shop, towards the door.

"Leaving already?" Katie said from the cash register, some snark hiding behind her words.

"Um, yeah. I'll see you," Julie said, quickly exiting, the bell chiming behind her. There was no way she would explain to Katie why she was gone. She suspected that Katie knew exactly why she was leaving. Julie left the shop, not knowing where to go. Back home? Having to face Josh with the news. Between the two of them, the only money they had was from the flower shop. Josh had been on a "job search" for over six months now, and she doubted that he would find one anytime soon. He would be furious.

So Julie wandered down the street, watching all the stores turn their signs to open for the beginning of the work day. The tears had stopped flowing, but she could still taste the salt on her lips. She knew that Josh would have to eventually know why they couldn't pay rent anymore, so she figured it was pointless in pretending she didn't just get fired. She crossed the street and walked to the small grocery store. They needed milk. The store was just opening, so she walked in. She found the milk and grabbed a gallon. They needed more groceries, but they couldn't exactly afford it. They couldn't afford beer either, but Julie picked up a twelve-pack out of the fridge anyway. She checked out, and went back to the subway.

At home, she walked to the door of their dingy little apartment that was crammed between two other equally rundown places. She unlocked the door and walked in, shutting the door softly behind her. The living room was to her right, where Josh was slumped on the couch, watching cartoons.

"Why the hell are you here?" Josh said, eyeing her from across the room.

"I um-"

"You got sacked, didn't you?" Josh said, standing up.

Julie walked to the kitchen and set the milk, beer, and her bag on the table.

"Julie? Is that what happened? You can't even keep a job at a place that sells plants?" Josh said, following her to the kitchen.

"Yeah, they let me go. I was late all the time, so they fired me." Julie ran her fingers through her hair, turning around to face Josh.

"I knew this would happen. No one can keep an idiot around for too long."

"That's not how it was, Josh," Julie stated.

"Sure. And what now? We can't afford to keep living here."

"We? Maybe if you had a job too, we wouldn't be totally screwed."

Josh took a step forward and pointed his finger at Julie's face.

"Don't you talk to me like that," he said, anger contorting his face.

"Sorry." Julie winced. "I can get another job,

it'll be fine." Julie went to move past Josh, but he grabbed her arm. Julie tried to yank it free, but he gripped harder.

"And in the meantime?" Josh said.

"You get a job," Julie answered, turning to look him in the eye. Josh threw her arm down and took a step closer. He turned and grabbed a beer and cracked the tab. He took a big swig before setting it down. Thinking the situation had simmered down, Julie went to hide in her room, like she usually did when he was like this.

"Don't you walk away from me. And never talk back," he hissed, getting close to her face.

"Josh, look, I'm sorry, I didn't me-" Julie gasped as Josh suddenly moved forward and shoved her by the shoulders. Hard. Julie stumbled back and tripped on her own feet, landing on her back and hitting her head on the floor. Ignoring the pain, she quickly sat up, pushed herself across the floor, trying to create space between them. Josh followed and hovered over her.

"Never again," Josh said.

He turned around, grabbed his beer, and walked slowly back to the living room, where the TV was still playing cartoons. Julie sat with her back against the wall, knees close to her chest. She could feel her heart beating fast, and she tried to take deep breaths to calm herself down, but there was no use. She heard Josh sit down in the next room. Julie closed her eyes and rested her head on the wall. It still hurt a lot, and she feared that she might have a concussion. She felt the back of her head with her hand where it hurt the worst. Her scalp felt sticky and warm, and when she pulled her hand back and looked at her palm, she saw her own crimson blood covering it.

She covered her mouth with her other hand and stifled a sob. Josh had done things like this before, but he never drew blood. She would get bruises from time to time, but nothing like this. Panic started to rush through her body. She stood up slowly and stepped backwards into the hall, keeping her eye on the living room. When she was out of sight, she ran into the room she shared with Josh.

Without thinking, letting the adrenaline guide her actions, she opened the closet doors and found her old suitcase buried under dirty laundry. She pulled it out and started shoving clothes into it, not caring what she was grabbing. Once it was full, she zipped it closed and stood up.

She looked around the room, trying to remember where she put her phone. After a few moments, she spotted it under the covers on the bed. She shoved it in her pocket and opened the drawer in the nightstand. She dug around and found a crumpled yellow sticky note with an address and a phone number she had written down a few months ago when Josh had first gotten physical with her. After that, though, she figured there wasn't really a way out. She didn't have any other choice. But now, she was desperate to find a way. She put the sticky note in her pocket with the phone. Julie's head throbbed, and she felt a little nauseous, but she didn't have time to worry about that quite yet.

Julie grabbed her suitcase and walked to the door. She peered down the hallway and didn't see Josh in the kitchen. She would have to make a run for it. She spotted her canvas tote on the table, next to the gallon of milk. She would have to grab that first. It had her wallet with her ID and credit card. Taking a deep breath, she took the first step out of the room and made a break for the kitchen. She moved quickly, but quietly. With her suitcase in one hand, she snatched her bag off the table and turned to walk to the front door. Her only way out. She walked swiftly past the living room.

"Hey! Where are you going?" Josh yelled from the couch. Julie paused, her hand resting on the doorknob.

"I'm leaving, Josh. For good," Julie said, turning and meeting his eye line. She stood a little straighter, but still held her breath.

"Oh yeah? And what are you going to do? Live on the streets?" he replied, leaning forward.

"I don't know. But what I do know is that I can't stay here any longer."

Josh leaned back into the couch and took a long pull from his beer can.

"Whatever, you'll be back."

Julie gritted her teeth and turned the doorknob. She paused for a moment.

"Bitch," Josh muttered under his breath from the couch.

Without any more second thoughts, Julie opened the door and stepped outside. She shut the door behind her and felt the warmth of the sunshine on her face.

*

Julie sits on the bench in this all too familiar subway. She watches the unfamiliar faces pass her by, not giving her a second thought. They are all too wrapped up in their own lives to notice her. She stares at her shoes, old ratty gray sneakers that she's owned since high school.

They are about a size too small, but the fabric stretched around her big toe hasn't given in to the pressure quite yet. Julie had stepped onto the train here every single day for the past year to go to the floral shop where she worked downtown. But that train is already long gone. Today is different for Julie. She has a different destination in mind. A hopeful destination. One that could possibly bring her to safety at last.

"Hey? Are you ok, miss?" A passerby stops and asks. "You look sick, do you need a hospital?"

"No, I'm ok. Thanks," Julie says, offering a small smile, surprised that someone took notice of her.

"Ok, you be safe," he says, looking doubtful.

"I will," Julie replies. He continues walking, giving a worried look over his shoulder.

Julie reaches into her pocket and pulls out the yellow sticky note and her phone. She hadn't dared to label the sticky note. Couldn't risk Josh finding it. A phone number is written on the top, in rushed handwriting. An address is scrawled beneath it. Julie unlocks her phone and dials the number. She puts the phone next to her ear, anxiously listening to the ringing on the other side. Whoever answers, she is confident that they can help. They can give her the space she needs to be safe, for now. Julie's nerves settle a bit at the thought. Safety. What a beautiful word.

***

JUNE, 2025 // ISSUE 02

Thorn & Bloom

Breaking the Cycle

a literary magazine

Thank you to everyone who submitted their work and entrusted us with their words—we are honoured to hold space for your voices.

A special heartfelt thank you to Rachel Lorraine, an unwavering inspiration to me personally as I have followed her work online and admired her courage to live in her most empowered self. I aspire to be just like that, so thank you for showing up and giving others permission to embody their most authentic selves.

CONTACT INFO:

www.redrosethorns.com
/
contact@redrosethorns.com
/
@redrosethorns

www.ingramcontent.com/pod-product-compliance
Lightning Source LLC
Chambersburg PA
CBHW041210100726
47911CB00017B/908

9798993122915